SILENT VOICES
from the Jungle

Wisdom of the Orangutan

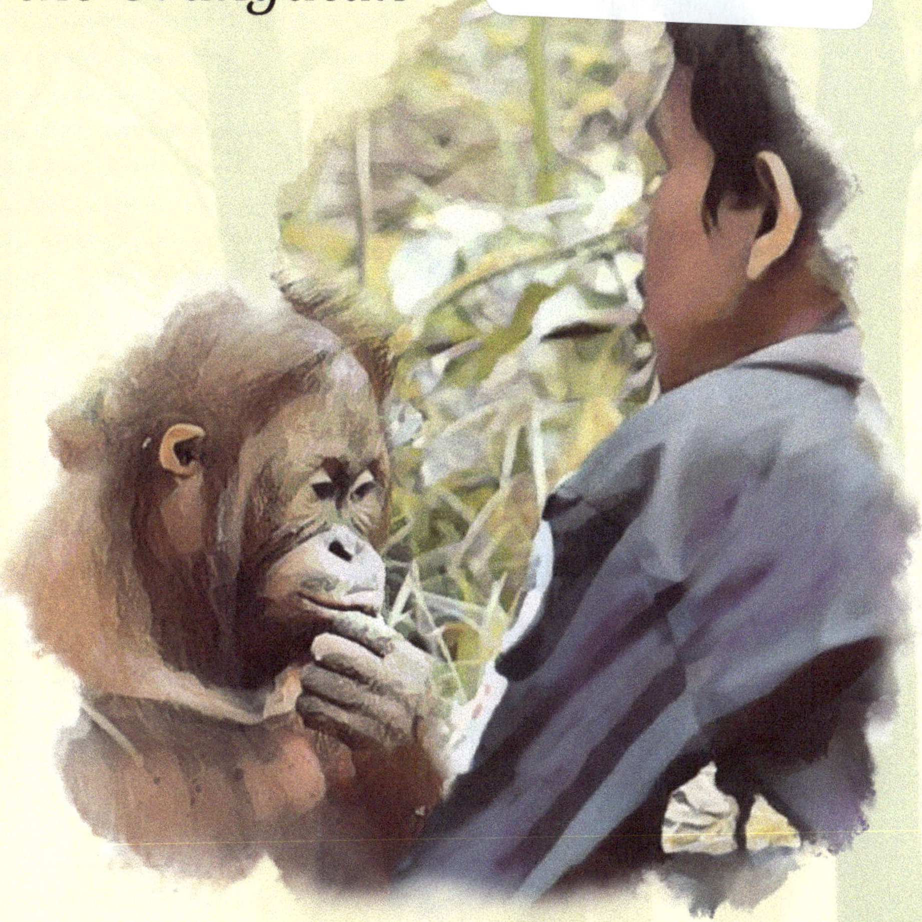

Jamartin Sihite

Jamartin Sihite

Silent Voices from the Jungle

Wisdom of the Orangutan

Silent Voices from the Jungle
Wisdom of the Orangutan

Author   : Jamartin Sihite
Cover Design   : Lalita Tri Adila
Photography   : Jamartin Sihite
Illustration   : Jamartin Sihite
Translation   : Sintha Nainggolan
Editor (English Version)   : Sintha Nainggolan
Editors (Indonesian Version) : Rukmi Wisnu Wardhani,
                                Jamartin Sihite,
                                Sintha Nainggolan

Paper   : Bookpaper
Size   : 14.5 x 20.5 cm
Pages   : xvi + 310

Edition I   : March 2025

Indeed, His blessing is nigh,

It's but a breath away.

For

The four Js who are (too) often overlooked,

who (often) come second to the orangutans,

and

the Beloved Intercessor of the family,

who now dwells with Him

From the Author

This collection of writings draws from my experiences, travel journals, challenges I have faced, as well as subjects for reflection, concerns, observations, and my hopes for my work in orangutan conservation and habitat preservation.

Friends, colleagues, and those who support orangutan conservation are likely familiar with the occasional commentaries I post on social media, such as Facebook and Instagram. However, this time, I have deliberately gathered and compiled them into this book.

Much happens during the course of conservation work, both in the field and behind the desk—whether attending meetings with conservation activists or engaging with policymakers, politicians, and their associates. Each of these is advancing the journey of orangutan conservation. The challenges we face require calm composure to address. As the wise say, one can understand politics without becoming a politician.

Notes from over a decade of experience serve as the foundation for these writings, expressed in a language far removed from the scientific. The goal is for the *"uneg-uneg,"* as we say in Indonesia—pent-up thoughts and feelings I have kept to myself—to be read, pondered, and, if possible, become part of the effort, albeit small, to foster better understanding and awareness about orangutan conservation for all, regardless of age or educational background. My hope is that the issues raised will become a collective consideration for us all.

Let us consider the issues together and engage in an open discussion on conservation, so that past mistakes are not repeated, and efforts, however less-than-stellar, can be improved to ensure the survival of endangered animals, particularly orangutans and their habitats.

Regardless of how small our actions may be, if done continually, they will create the impact we hope for to support life on Earth—both for the present and the future, for our children and grandchildren.

This Silent Voice is more of a personal travel journal; therefore, please excuse any shortcomings within it. If there are incomplete lessons and insights here and there, may the baton of the learnings I hope for and dream of be passed on as a relay task for those who embrace such challenges.

Finally, the Silent Voice on a silent road is full of imperfections, and it's a journey that requires perseverance. It is important that the messages of these silent voices be heard, even if it means taking the silent road.

Happy Reading!

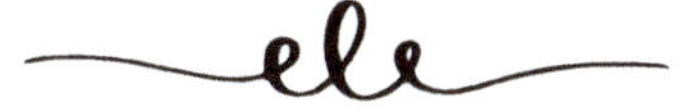

Table of Contents

Essays & Musings

Dialogues with the Orangutans

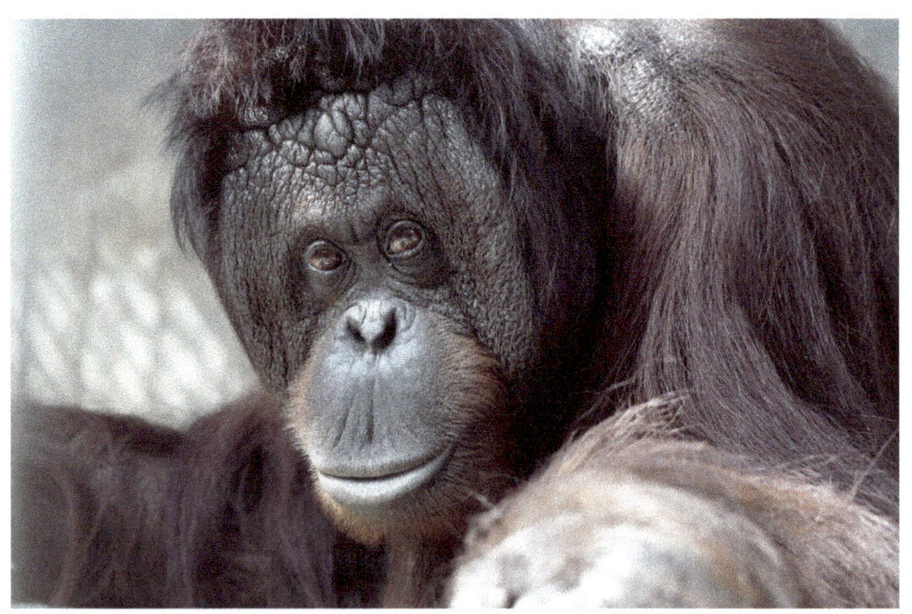

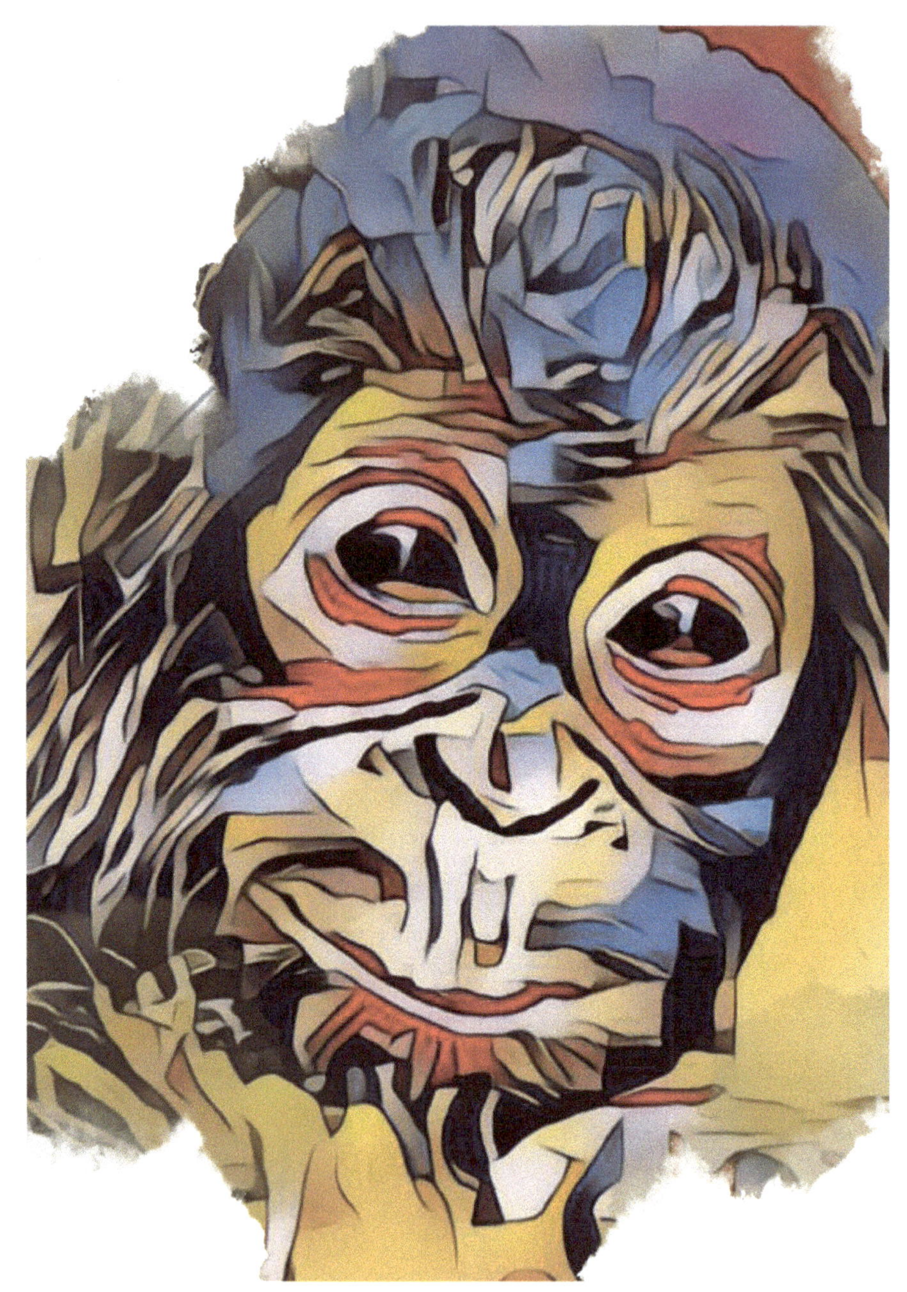

The forest whispered to the Divine,
"God, grant us a companion,
A loyal steward and steadfast guardian."
And so, He gifted them the orangutans.

-RWW-

Chapter 1

A Smile from Heaven

At the end of each year, the Borneo Orangutan Survival Foundation (BOSF) reintroduces rehabilitated orangutans to their rightful home in the forest as a Christmas gift. Releasing orangutans into a remote forest is both challenging and costly. The difficulty stems from the fact that the forest where we release these orangutans has minimal infrastructure and remains underdeveloped. The lack of accessibility to these areas drives up costs, making the journey a strain on our finances.

However, returning these displaced orangutans to live among the trees means restoring their precious lives in accordance with God's inherent plan. The exhaustion from the long, arduous journey to the chosen release site is quickly forgotten as we witness the joyful, smiling faces of the freed orangutans when the doors to their cages are opened.

Once the orangutans leave their cages, they are not simply abandoned in the forest. The post-release monitoring program, which begins right after the release, is vital to ensuring their successful adaptation. Our team continues to monitor them, and this requires significant effort—often involving metaphorical, and sometimes literal blood, sweat, and tears.

The work of the monitoring team is grueling—they certainly sweat as they climb cliffs and descend ravines, which are part of their daily routine. There are times when members of the monitoring team are brought to tears, faced with the difficult choice of either climbing an impossible cliff or losing track of the orangutan they are monitoring. At other times, they return to the monitoring hut with blood from injuries resulting from falling or slipping off a rocky cliff.

But are they deterred from the task at hand? No, they simply smile or laugh self-deprecatingly at their own missteps. These joyful smiles—from both the team and the freed orangutans—are priceless; they are like smiles from heaven.

One day, as I sat on a boulder by the riverbank, I heard a voice: "Hi there, why are you smiling to yourself?" It was Beni, the newly released orangutan.

At the time, the team and I were relaxing and having lunch by the river after tracking Beni's progress following his release from the open cage. I was smiling as I imagined Beni's joyful grin—the smile of a free orangutan—as he roamed freely in the forest, the home that God had designated for orangutans. Beni was apparently watching us in the forest and eager to greet us with his genuine friendliness.

"I am smiling because I remember the beaming smile on your face as you climbed the tree after leaving the cage,"

I replied with a chuckle. "It was as if you were sharing that smile with the entire world."

"Of course! A smile is like a candle," Beni explained. "Thousands of candles can be lit from just one. And happiness never diminishes when it is shared. As you share your happiness with us, we return the favor by sharing ours with all who have freed us into our natural habitat."

"Releasing orangutans back into the wild isn't easy, my friend, it's hard!" I replied. "But we always try to do it with a smile."

"If you feel your burden is heavier than others', it's because God knows you're more capable than others of carrying it," said Beni cheerfully. "We orangutans love your smiling demeanor, and we understand that sometimes people choose to smile rather than explain why they are sad or frustrated."

"Because, at the end of this endeavor, our deepest hope is to be satisfied with our work and to share a smile together. That's why we make sure to be thorough and not rush the process in our release preparation," I said to Beni.

"That's right, my friend. We should learn to stay calm. I've regretted being hasty in the past. We should also learn to manage anger because what follows it is usually regret," Beni commented, looking into my eyes with a bright smile.

"So, in that case, let's bring that smile of joy and happiness from heaven to earth, wherever we are, shall we, Beni?"

"Absolutely. Smiling is the easiest way to build a connection, and a genuine smile is something money can't buy, my friend. As Mother Teresa once said, 'A smile is the beginning of love,'" said Beni, meeting my gaze.

My mind immediately catalogued the many challenges we have faced in orangutan conservation. "But sometimes, we still experience disappointment and heartbreak, Beni," I said, reflecting on the difficulties of this work. Perhaps it is the darker side of my humanity that drives my need for validation, as the strain of this job often makes us less cheerful—and, in turn, less willing to smile.

"Unfortunately, whether you like it or not, it's pain that matures us," Beni replied. "Forget the hurt, and forgive those who caused it. But don't forget those who love you today. Disappointment is simply God's way of saying, 'I have something better for you.' So, there's no reason not to grace us with your smile, my friend. A smile is contagious. Your one smile can encourage those around you to do the same. Isn't a smile the shortest distance between two people?" Beni said wisely, just before he slowly disappeared behind the lush foliage.

At that moment, even though I hadn't finished my meal, my heart and mind were already full, simply from talking and smiling with Beni. Yes, the brightest smile of an orangutan is seen when he is at home, free to roam his natural habitat.

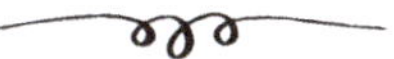

Life is a winding road, with twists and turns, hurdles and setbacks along the way. Problems in life may not be easy to solve, but it's best to keep on smiling while dealing with them. No matter how difficult life gets, we must keep our lightheartedness and not hesitate to do the right thing. And if we want to soar into the sky, shouldn't we first unload the burdens in our hearts? Remember, complaining only weighs us down, while gratitude leads us to the path of ease.

Our elders say that life is like a mirror. When we smile, the world will smile back at you. No instruments in the world can measure the warmth of a smile. Even when life provides a hundred reasons to cry, we should show it a thousand more reasons to smile. As Ali bin Abu Talib once said, "Smile, even though your heart is bleeding."

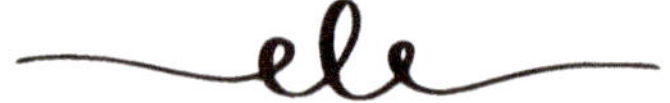

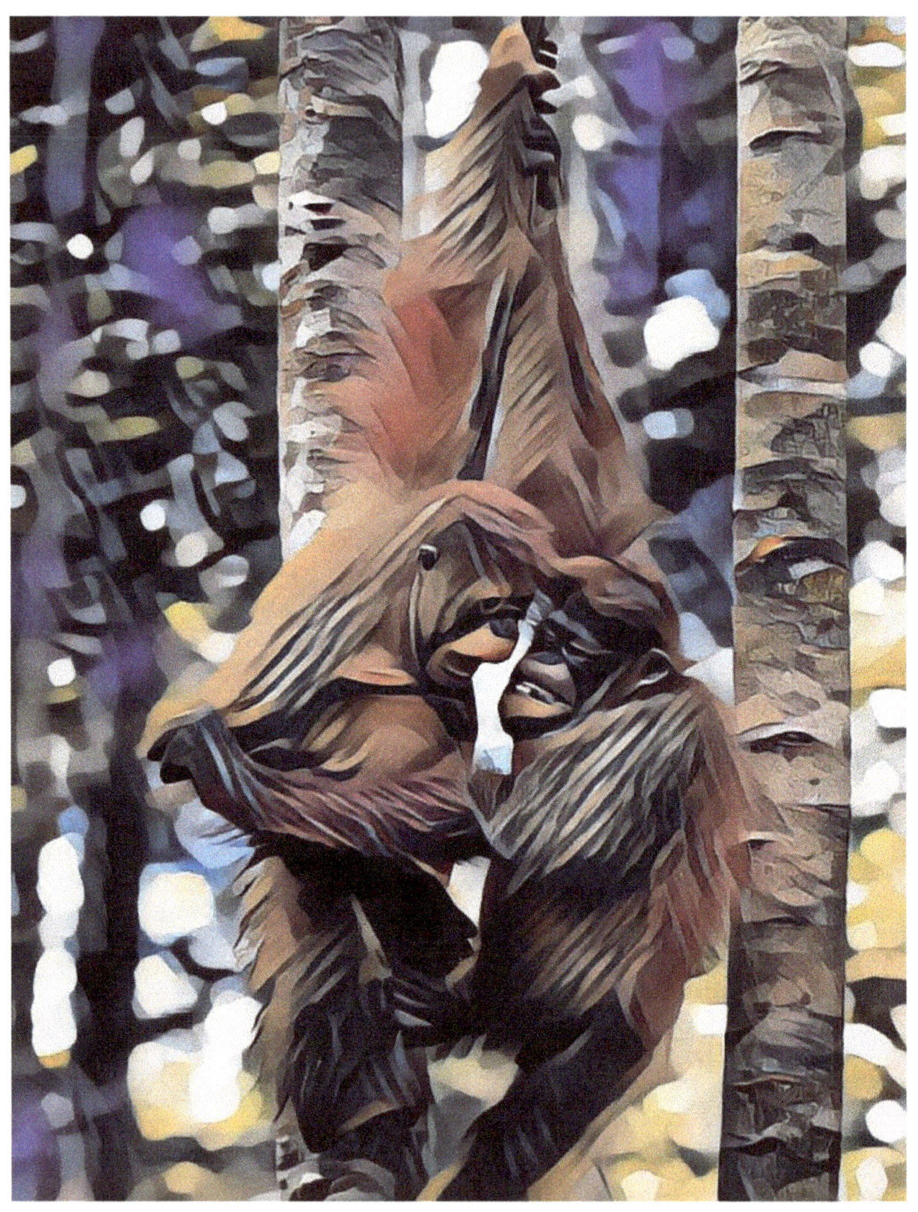

"Becoming better every day
is not determined by others,
but by our efforts,
to strive and make it happen."

Chapter 2

Better Every Day

The first time I entered an orangutan rehabilitation center, my immediate thought was, "Wow! How extraordinary is this foundation, to be able to care for hundreds of orangutans! No other zoo in the world houses as many in their facilities."

Filled with awe, I strolled around the grounds, watching the orangutans in their enclosures. As I observed these magnificent creatures, I was suddenly startled by a voice greeting me. I looked around but saw no one else—only a row of cages filled with orangutans. Thinking I had misheard, I resumed walking. Just as I was enjoying the silence, the voice spoke again, "Hey, no need to be confused. It's us, the orangutans. We're just saying hello to you."

I carefully scanned a row of cages where many orangutans were intently watching me, gripping the iron bars of their cages. My heart raced. I took deep breaths to steady myself. As I regained my composure, I walked over to a large tree to gather my thoughts. While still in disbelief, I tried to process what had just happened. Was I hallucinating? Or were these orangutans trying to communicate with me? If so, I decided I would listen closely.

I had nothing to lose, so I responded as calmly as I could, "Alright, here I am, and I'm listening."

"Think about your premise of rehabilitation," said the voice. "I think it's time you reevaluate your beliefs. The purpose of having orangutans in this center is to teach us the skills so that one day we can return to living freely among the trees in the forest, not be confined to cages."

I remained silent, trying to digest what the speaker was saying.

As faint as a whisper in the wind, the voice of the orangutan was heard again: "Do you understand why we are in this situation? It is because those of you who care for us orangutans hold high opinions of yourselves. 'Look how wonderful we are,' you say. 'We can care for hundreds of orangutans in the cages!' Yet the truth is, we find ourselves in our current predicament because our homes were destroyed by humans. While it's understandable that you feel a sense of pride about helping, there is no denying that we remain confined."

He paused before continuing, "But you know, when you already believe you're the best, your willingness to evolve and change will cease. You stop making an effort to improve. Why even bother thinking about how to become better when you already consider yourself the best? That's why these cages will never be emptied, and we orangutans will never return to our homes in the forest!" he said indignantly.

I gasped. What the orangutan said struck me like a thunderbolt. I suddenly recalled my late father's advice: "Don't be afraid of making small progress, because that is far better than staying still and not making any changes at all. It is important to know where you're going and not be swayed by everyone else's opinion. Finishing a task is always better than striving for perfection."

As I reflected on his words, I realized the truth in what the orangutan had said. When we believe we're already the best, we resist change, and as a result, our efforts to improve come to a halt. A civilization is constantly evolving because people grow dissatisfied with the progress they've made. Therefore, it is natural that we strive to do better, improving ourselves each day, as if tomorrow were our last, and we were to face Him, our Creator.

The orangutan continued, "My friend, we in the forest are accustomed to self-evaluation. It is a way of assessing what you have accomplished based on the efforts you put in. You can also use it to reflect on your abilities and the quality of your work."

"However, self-evaluation shouldn't be limited to times when your achievements fall short of your expectations or when you experience failure," he reminded me. "It is equally important to assess yourself when you succeed."

"Failure often reveals areas where you have shortcomings or mistakes that need attention," he said. "On the other hand, success can breed overconfidence, even arrogance, causing you to become complacent with your accomplishments—and that can lead to mistakes. So, it's important to remain aware of your situation, not only during challenging times, but also when you experience success or joy."

"Self-evaluation will help you better understand the good and bad aspects of life. By examining your experiences, you will recognize shortcomings as mistakes to correct quickly, while positive qualities are virtues to preserve and cultivate. Understanding these will make you much wiser in navigating life," he said thoughtfully.

"As a result, you will become more adept at positioning yourself, reading situations, and responding to both the positive and negative aspects of life. Improvement doesn't come from belittling others, but from focusing on bettering yourself. By doing so, you will be more mindful of your actions and the decisions you make throughout your life's journey," explained the orangutan.

I was impressed. "Wow, this is a valuable lesson for me! We must continually work on improving ourselves, don't we? One can learn much more from facing defeat than from experiencing victory. So, in essence, your message to us humans is: 'Don't just pray when the rain comes but also remember to pray when the sun shines brightly.' That's what I understand from your advice."

The orangutan laughed after hearing what I said, "That's right, my friend. However, improvement requires a continuous process; It doesn't happen in the blink of an eye. This is why it's called a learning process."

He fell quiet for a moment, then continued, "A long time ago, while we were gazing at the moon from our nest, the wind whispered a Chinese proverb: *'bù néng yīkǒu chī chéng gè pàngzi.'* It means 'it is impossible to eat a single meal and become fat', or, in other words: we cannot achieve something spontaneously or at lightning speed. This proverb teaches us the importance of patience and reminds us that everything in life involves a process. It's much like my own learning journey when I was a baby, held in my mother's arms. At the time, she taught me how to hang and swing from tree branches, whereas today, I've learned nothing but how to sit glumly, holding the iron bars of my cage. So keep striving for better results. Don't chase quick successes, and don't forget to enjoy and be grateful for the process you experience along the way!" he said cheerfully.

"Wow, that's just like the motto of one of the soccer teams in England," I said. "Dare to do better every day. *'Audere est facere'*—courage is proven through action."

Then, faintly, I heard the orangutan continue, "There is an Indian proverb that says: 'Your future doesn't rely on the lines of your palm, because even those without hands still have a future.' So, our everyday improvement is not determined by others, but by our efforts to make it happen."

Make an effort to improve every day, so we can confidently say that today is better than yesterday. Strict adherence to the best set of guidelines can trap us in complacency and vanity, slowing down innovation and creativity. Once again, the orangutan has taught me an important concept and philosophy of life that is worth following.

To improve ourselves, let's focus on the steps we can take, rather than believing in superstition or waiting for the 'right' moment. The best time to act is now, not later. Trust that by taking the first step, we move closer to our dreams. However, daily improvement cannot be achieved instantly; it is a process that requires both perseverance and hope.

Life is always filled with trials and tribulations, and it is these challenges that add richness and color. How we handle, navigate, and overcome challenges is far more important than the challenges themselves. Indeed, the process of problem-solving gives deeper meaning to our human existence. Isn't life truly about the process of living?

Learning isn't limited to schools or confined to textbooks. Nature itself is a teacher, guiding us toward a deeper understanding of life's purpose. Through nature, God reveals the meaning of life. And this time, God has sent the orangutans to be my teachers.

I sincerely hope my experiences and the wisdom I have gained can also benefit your learning journey, my fellow humans.

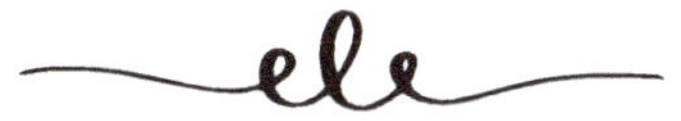

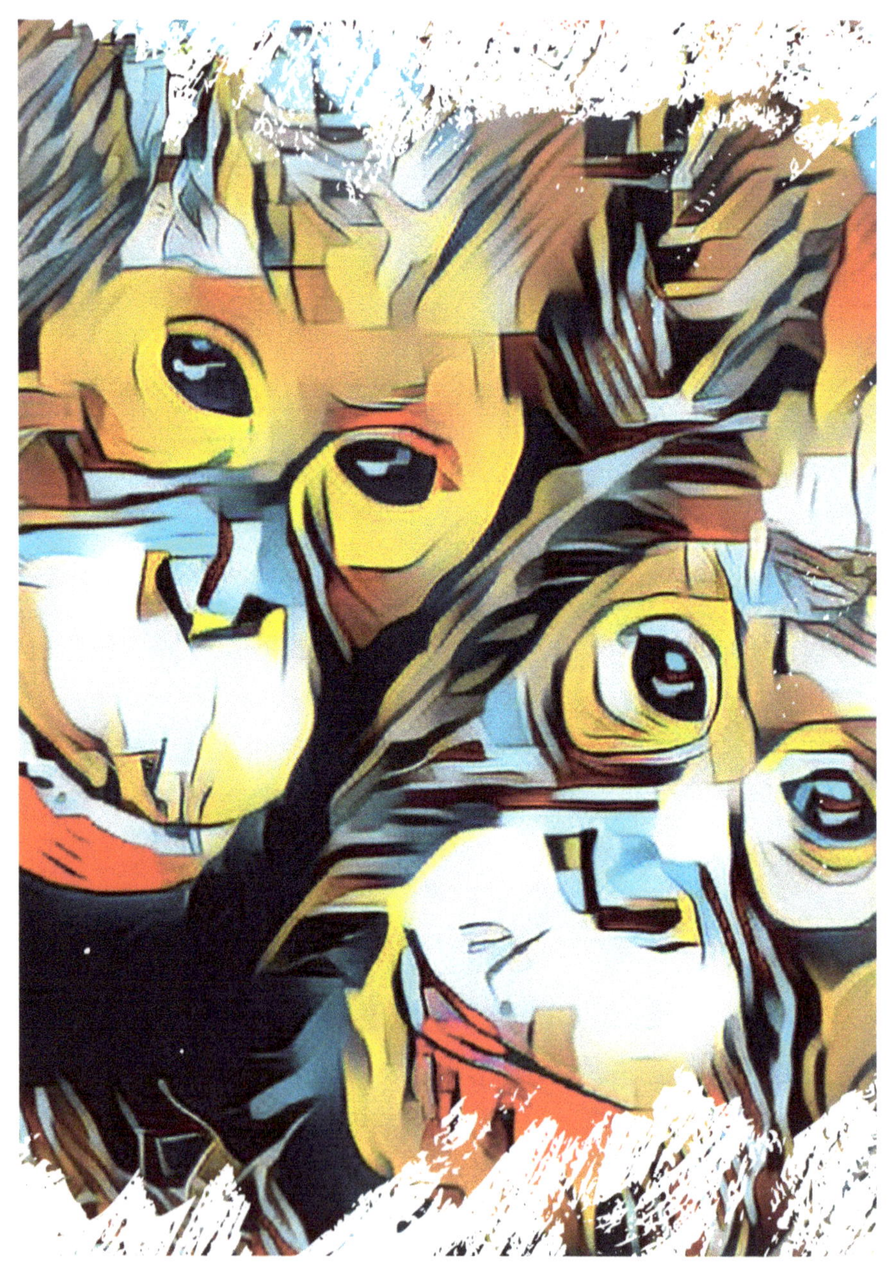

If they destroy our forests,
And we slowly perish,
What will you do...?

-RWW-

Chapter 3

Among the Trees, Without the Forest

A long time ago, my team and I ventured into the forest to survey potential sites for releasing orangutans. It was an arduous journey, as we traveled hundreds of kilometers into a remote area where infrastructure was almost non-existent. One night, while staying in a temporary hut with a tarpaulin roof and an earthen floor, my mind wandered aimlessly. The tranquility of nature and the sounds of nocturnal animals kept me company throughout the night.

Although finding a suitable forest that met all the requirements for re-homing a fully rehabilitated orangutan was challenging, what troubled me most that night was the future of the orangutans who could not be released. In my mind's eye, I envisioned enclosures filled with orangutans who could never return to the wild—hundreds who would remain captive for the rest of their lives. What happened to them wasn't really their fault; it was the result of misguided human attitudes and behaviors.

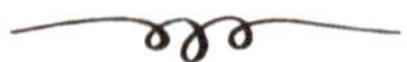

Some orangutans at the Borneo Orangutan Survival Foundation's (BOSF) rehabilitation center show slow progress in their rehabilitation programs. They struggle to keep up with the others in developing the necessary skills and behaviors to survive in the wild. This difficulty is generally caused by spending too much time with humans at a young age.

Other orangutans suffer from infectious diseases such as tuberculosis or hepatitis B and C, which can recur at any time. These diseases pose a transmission risk, and infected orangutans could potentially spread them to others, especially within the larger wild orangutan population. As a result, those suffering from these diseases are isolated and cared for in a special complex at the rehabilitation center.

Another group of orangutans that cannot be released into the wild are those with physical limitations or impairments, such as missing limbs or blindness.

All orangutans in these categories are considered "unreleasable," and their numbers are in the hundreds. While the goal—and the expectation—of orangutan conservation, particularly in rehabilitation centers, is to rehabilitate and eventually release all rescued orangutans, unfortunately, this target is not always achievable due to the reasons mentioned.

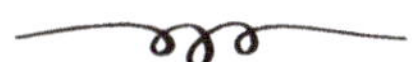

On that dark night, as I listened to the rhythmic drips of rain and the distant sounds of nocturnal animals, my thoughts turned to Iqbal, a male orangutan who inhabited one of the enclosures at the BOSF rehabilitation center in Nyaru Menteng, Central Kalimantan. I couldn't help but imagine his thoughts and feelings. What must it be like for him to spend years in a cage with limited space to move?

Then Iqbal's voice greeted me, "Hello, my friend, what is bothering your mind right now? What problems are you trying to solve?"

"I am pondering your situation, Iqbal. Currently, you and dozens, even hundreds, of orangutans are trapped in your cages, and unable to be released into the wild. And it is all our fault," I replied dejectedly, as I sat cross-legged on the portable folding bed made of burlap sack.

"Haven't you ever been stuck in the mud, unable to get out? Or spent a night in the forest, feeling as though your world had stopped and you were isolated?" he asked. "Did you stop trying to escape? Of course not. You kept looking for ways to free yourself from the mud. So, using that as an analogy: never stop learning, because life never stops teaching you."

I ignored Iqbal's reply. "However, you orangutans were made for the forest, to live freely and fulfill God's commands. By living in cages, you lose the very essence of why you were created. That's why you orangutans belong in the trees," I insisted.

"Rehabilitating unreleasable orangutans like us to the point where we can live among the trees and be free from cages is no easy feat. But remember, my friend, although life is oftentimes difficult, we simply need to show that we are stronger than the challenges we face," Iqbal said, responding to my protest.

He paused for a moment, then continued. "Why don't you think about how we could still live among the trees in the forest, even in a small area with territorial boundaries, like a refuge or sanctuary? Although we can't be released into the wild, we would feel more dignified living among the trees in this way, rather than being caged for life.

"Iqbal, you realize that the right of sanctuary is an ancient judicial concept, don't you? It's when a person who is persecuted or mistreated in their homeland can be protected by another sovereign authority, right?" I replied.

"Indeed. Wouldn't you consider confinement in a cage to be a form of mistreatment? This way, you can still free us from these cages, even if it isn't returning us to the forest. Aren't you familiar with the concept of a 'wildlife sanctuary'—a safe haven—where endangered animals can live and find refuge?"

Iqbal's statement jolted my mind. A sanctuary! For those who can no longer return to the wild! Could this be the essence of the saying: "When the world says, 'Give up,' Hope whispers, 'Try one more time.'?" Let's establish a sanctuary, a safe space, for those who can no longer be released into the wild, although executing the idea would inevitably come with pros and cons, and its own controversies—such as how having the orangutans in an island-reserve within a forested, but restricted, area would be any different from living in cages. In both cases, they are unable to roam freely, unlike in a true forest.

Then, out of the blue, he added, "Listen to what Martin Luther King Jr. once said, my friend: 'The ultimate measure of a person is not in his stance in times of comfort and convenience, but in his stance in challenge and controversy.'"

I was stunned by his words. It was as though he could read my unspoken thoughts and concerns about building this new sanctuary for orangutans who carry human diseases, who have physical disabilities, and for those who can't be released back into the wild.

"Allow us orangutans who can't return to the forest to live among the trees, rather than behind bars and walls. In an island sanctuary, however small it may be, we could still enjoy the night with the moon, the stars, and the vast sky. That way, we could experience peace. Despite our handicaps, we still have the right to enjoy God's love, don't we? And the beauty of nature is a testament to God's love for us," Iqbal continued, explaining his hopes.

Even though Iqbal and his orangutan friends cannot be released into the wilderness, they still have the right to live among trees and enjoy the magnificence of nature. For it is from nature that we learn to be grateful to our Creator.

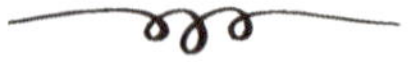

In this life, we often encounter those with physical limitations. They, too, are creations of the Almighty, designed for a specific purpose. We, who do not have physical restrictions, also have other limitations; in fact, everything in this world has its limits, because only He, who owns Life, is able to do everything without limit. This Owner of Life has given us the universe and nature, along with valuable lessons through the beauty of the rainbow and its many colors.

Because of this, let us make accepting differences be a beautiful process of creating harmony, rather than a point of contention—or worse, a means to demean others. As Einstein said, "Look deep into nature and you will understand everything better." Learning from His creations will expand our souls.

Let us build a sanctuary for orangutans who cannot return to the forest; they deserve to live in the trees. It is our duty to protect the dignity of orangutans and allow them to live freely in nature.

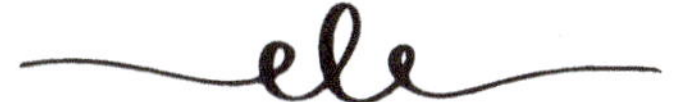

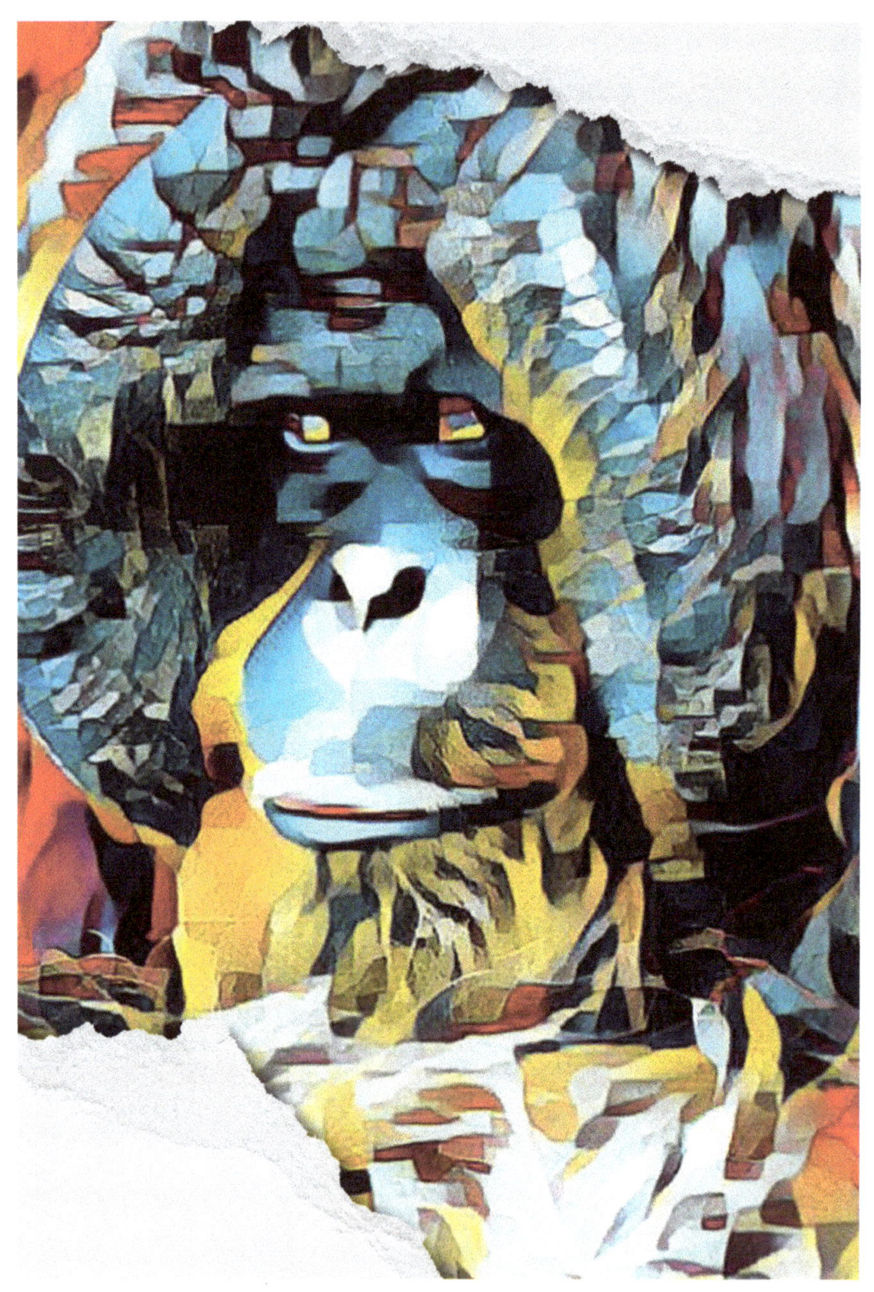

We can enjoy the warmth,
For we've known the chill of cold.
We can appreciate the light,
For we've felt what it's like to be in the dark.

Chapter 4

Turmoil

One evening, Jakarta was drenched in a downpour. The air conditioning, left running during that rainy afternoon, made the room feel much colder than it actually was, despite being set to only 23 degrees Celsius. Yet, the chilly temperature seemed powerless to alleviate the 'overheating' that had taken root in my mind. Imagine—three back-to-back meetings in one day, each addressing topics that only worsened my mood.

While it is true that, in life, anyone can feel a range of emotions—such as happiness, sadness, or anger—within the same day, I would probably blame my irritability that day on sheer exhaustion. When asked whether my feelings that evening stemmed from physical or emotional fatigue, I couldn't provide a clear answer. All I knew was that my mind felt weary. The accusation that I wasn't performing well at my job caused my mood to plunge into deep gloom. Throughout that afternoon, I found myself feeling grumpy, annoyed, irritated, and too unmotivated to engage in any activities.

Although I conducted the online meetings from the comfort of my home, I was still in turmoil. For a long time, I sat in silence, staring at the energetic splatter of raindrops that seemed to greet me from the other side of my office window. Then, I heard the faint voice of Bujang, an orangutan living at the island sanctuary in Samboja, East Kalimantan, calling out to me. He had been rescued from a circus in Tanjung Pinang, Riau Islands, where he had been a victim of the exploitation of wild animals for entertainment.

"Hey, friend, what's with the frown? I can feel the energy of anger and annoyance radiating off you."

"I just finished a marathon of meetings, Bujang. Imagine this—three online meetings in one day! To make matters worse, each one came with unpleasant surprises, causing my mood to spiral into chaos," I replied, scowling, my eyes still following the rhythmic drops of rain on the window, hoping the soothing sound of the rain would calm my heart and wash away my annoyance.

"Would you mind telling me what's got you so upset?" Bujang asked. "You seem quite agitated."

"I just had a heated discussion with my colleagues. They insisted they were in the right and indirectly accused us of not doing our job properly. They unfairly blamed us for tasks we weren't equipped to handle, like enforcing the law. They also demanded that we apologize for things we didn't do. On top of that, they insisted that we befriend those who had committed past transgressions—people with blood on their hands, who had greatly contributed to environmental damage. Altogether, this has taken a toll on my emotional state," I replied hotly.

"Calm down, my friend. We orangutans would like to ask: are you and your colleagues truly without sin? This reminds me of a story from the Bible, where Jesus confronted a group of Jews who were judging a woman caught in adultery. Jesus picked up a stone and said, 'Let anyone among you who is without sin be the first to throw this stone at her.' The profound meaning of that story is that, fundamentally, all humans are sinners, isn't it? So why are you so upset?" he said softly, as though he could feel my frustration.

He then continued more firmly, "If your fellow conservation workers make accusations against you, don't retaliate with another accusation. It's like the saying from Lesotho: 'A war among grasshoppers is a feast for the crows.' I hope you understand what I'm saying, my friend," he finished sagely.

"Is it wrong if I'm upset and not in a good mood?" I said, clenching my fist tightly, hoping that act would crush all the turmoil souring my mind and heart.

"Hey, take it easy, my friend. Let's look at the facts. In this organization, you and your colleagues come from different backgrounds and cultures, which becomes especially clear when you interact with those from abroad. Think about it: the language you speak, the cultural norms you follow, and the values you hold aren't the same as theirs. All of these contribute to differing viewpoints," he explained.

"Now, understand that every life is a story, and your colleagues are part of your own story in conservation. So why not weave gratitude into the fabric of your experience? Expressing gratitude will make your journey more positive. Plus, apologizing for something you didn't do won't hurt you. It may even reduce tension and foster better communication. After all, you can't solve problems without discussing them, can you?" he added.

"But asking me to befriend someone who has sinned or committed an offense is a mistake!" I said, exasperated.

"Hahaha, right now, you're already judging your colleagues as being in the wrong. So how about this: let's leave it to God to judge sins, and let the justice system handle the law violations they committed. Your job, and the job of all God's creations, is to hate the sin, but not the sinner. I admit, it's not easy—it requires a process. But by doing so, you encourage them to become better. However, if it makes your life difficult, unfortunately, it is a shared consequence you should have considered before involving yourself in conservation work, especially with orangutans and habitat preservation. Besides, is there anything easy about conservation problems?" Bujang said with a smile.

He then continued, "We orangutans need those of you working in conservation to avoid withdrawing into a state of sullenness, petulance, or irritability—or, as they say in Indonesian, '*mutung*' and '*bete*'. Maintain a joyful heart, and find joy in walking the silent path. Remember, my friend, there are many unattainable things in this world. Observe a butterfly when you are in the forest; it's always just out of reach. Chase it and it will escape you. You won't be able to catch it. But if you sit quietly (and reflect on the journey of your orangutan work in the meantime), the butterfly may just land on you without you having to chase it," he explained wisely.

"But, these colleagues are also my friends. They're important to me," I protested, though my tone had noticeably softened. I think my ego was just resisting the change of heart.

Bujang responded with amusement, "My friend, today's millennials in Indonesia describe friendship with the rhyme *'Pertemanan itu bagai kepompong, kadang kepo, kadang rempong'*. It means that friendship (*pertemanan*) can sometimes be nosy (*kepo*), and at other times, fussy and complicated (*rempong*)," he explained deftly, translating the current Indonesian slang. "You will know who your real friends are when you're experiencing hardships."

"But remember, don't live with regret, wasting too much time and missing opportunities by being caught up in your inner turmoil. Be patient if the Creator hasn't answered your prayers yet. And remember, you are not the only one praying," he reminded me.

I remained silent as I pondered Bujang's words. His reasoning was so sound that there was no room for argument.

"So, always be prepared for life's unpleasant side, but be happy and maintain a joyful heart. As happy as I was when I was still in the cage. Don't think for a moment that I didn't experience stress when my space to move was restricted by iron bars. And that's not even counting the trauma I endured from being taken by irresponsible poachers to Tanjung Pinang, where I was used as an entertainment animal, or the devastation of watching my mother being killed right before my eyes. Despite all that, I didn't give up hope. I always held on to hope, just like it says in our favorite song." Bujang then sang a verse from the song:

> *Keep giving me hope for a better day*
> *Keep giving me love to find a way*
> *Through this heaviness I feel*
> *I just need someone to say, everything's okay*

"Remember, my friend, your turmoil won't save the orangutans in the slightest. Also, remember that life is often ironically twisted. Sometimes, the very people you're willing to protect from bullets turn out to be the ones holding the gun. But that's the essence of friendship: we are willing to defend them, even if it hurts us in the end. And if that eventuality happens, always remember what you are really fighting for, the beaming smiles of my friends, the orangutans who are now free in the forest."

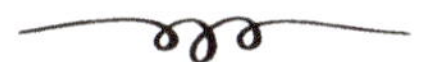

"We must accept finite disappointment, but never lose infinite hope," said Martin Luther King Jr. Hope is the reason warriors are willing to lay down their lives. Inner turmoil is not healthy for anyone, so it must be managed. Sometimes, this feeling makes us angry, and we must understand that it's easier to lash out at someone than to communicate that our feelings have been hurt, or that they have upset us.

Bujang reminded me—and you, too, dear readers—that life plays out in contrast. We appreciate warmth because we've experienced cold. We value light because we've been in darkness. Similarly, we can experience joy, because we've known turmoil.

So, don't waste your time being conflicted for any reason. People tend to care only when it's already too late. Let's cultivate the habit of saying "thank you." Although 'thank you' is one of the easiest phrases to say in any language, it has become a commodity that is increasingly rare in today's society.

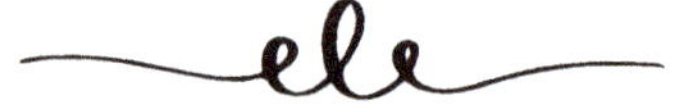

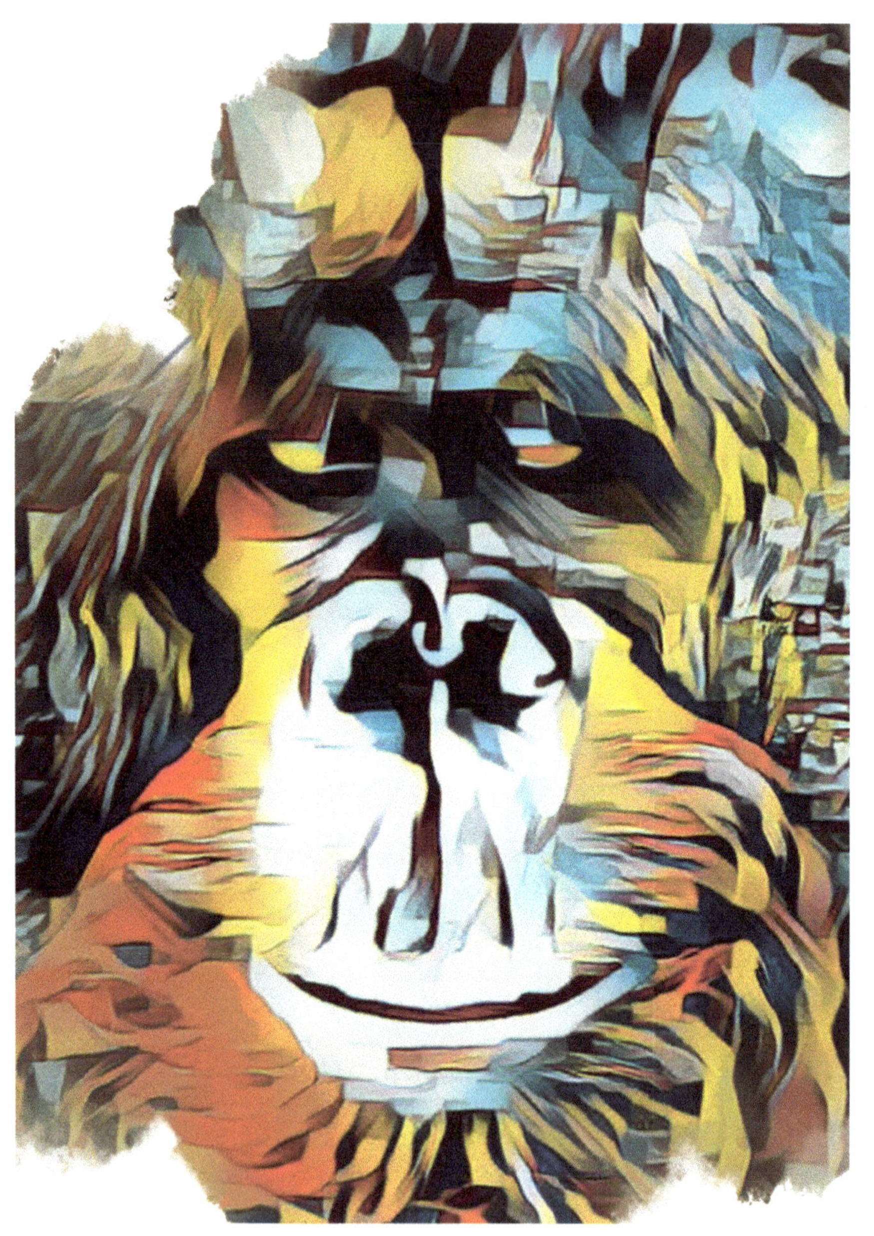

Greeted by sunlight through gaps in the shady canopy,
Once I lived without bars,
Gazing at the moon and the twinkling stars,
Before falling asleep, embraced by the warmth of the nest.

Is there a forest for me to return to?

-RWW-

Chapter 5

If Only

One day, as I was heading back to Jakarta after visiting the orangutan rehabilitation center, I walked past a restaurant at the airport on my way to the lounge to wait for my flight. Without meaning to, my gaze fell on a diner sitting at a table, overflowing with plates piled high with delicious dishes, eagerly devouring his meal. I couldn't help but think, '*Wow, what a big appetite this guy has.*'

Even when I was at the airport lounge, for some reason, the image of the diner and his food-laden table lingered in my mind. It wasn't that I envied his appetite, but that scene made me wonder: '*If only that diner hadn't eaten so much, he could have donated the money he didn't spend to help us feed orangutans in captivity. Even better, if only we could get just 10% of all Indonesians to genuinely care about orangutan conservation. If only, if only...*'

While waiting for my flight, my mind drifted from one "if-only" to another, until it was interrupted by a greeting from Kopral, an armless orangutan living at our site in Samboja Lestari, East Kalimantan. Despite his disability,

Kopral had an extraordinary spirit and zest for life. Both of his arms were amputated after they had rotted from the electric burns he sustained. He had once been kept by someone in a cage, and in an attempt to escape through an electric wire on a utility pole, he was electrocuted, suffering severe burns. Later, his owner abandoned him at the rehabilitation center, leaving him in a cardboard box at the doorstep.

"So, why is your mind full of wishful 'if-onlys,' my friend?" Kopral asked. "Even though my arms were amputated after they rotted from the horrific burns, I didn't dwell on such thoughts. I should be the one lamenting, 'If only I still had my arms,' or 'If only I could have been released,' or 'I wish...' But be careful with 'if-onlys,' because they don't help you solve problems."

"Well, I was thinking—if only we had enough funds, we could have more forest to manage as orangutan habitat. With sufficient funding, we could also train our staff to build capacity, increase their knowledge and skills, and improve their attitudes and behavior. We could also allocate funds to educate the public and raise awareness about orangutan conservation. More funding would also mean we could strengthen law enforcement. Unfortunately, it's nothing more than a utopian dream," I said, trailing off into a whisper, feeling ashamed of how little we could do. If only all our wishes were fulfilled, we could have done better work. But that is not the reality. In conservation, we often face uncertain circumstances, limited resources, and unique challenges.

"You sound like someone in love, yearning to be together, saying, 'If only you were here,' to express your feelings," teased Kopral gently. "But remember that if you're ready to fall in love, you're also ready to get your heart broken. Not every love story ends with a happy ending, you know. It's the same with your work, your life with the forest, and the orangutans. Come on, stop dwelling on the 'if-onlys.' They're poison," Kopral said vehemently.

"If only my colleagues supported our work," I muttered, ignoring Kopral's reprimand to banish 'if-only' from my mind and let go of the wishful thinking that, according to him, poisons our work.

"We are often unaware that we place expectations on those we cannot rely on," Kopral commented. "Let me give you an example. Why does someone look back on his achievements? It is not to relive the past, but usually to motivate himself to do better. It's the same with love. Love isn't about ownership; it's about sincerity and detachment—or *'ikhlas,'* as we say in Indonesia," Kopral reminded me once again not to dwell on wishful thinking.

"But is it wrong to expect better conditions, so that our work to protect nature can be more effective and easier?" I replied, stubbornly insisting that using the phrase 'if-only' wasn't entirely unjustifiable, and that it wasn't poison in this thorny job—a profession, as one of our country's presidents put it, that makes us "walk the silent path."

"The reason you brood over 'if-onlys' is your desire for a perfect outcome, where all conditions are favorable," Kopral explained. "But remember, a warrior rises in an unjust and imperfect world, and he doesn't allow himself to get caught up in wishful thinking. A warrior sacrifices—not for the fame of recognition, but because he believes in what he is fighting for, champions his ideals, and stands firm in the goodness of his cause. He doesn't wait until everything is in place before taking action; he does what needs to be done and constantly strives to improve," Kopral admonished me with his sharp, steady gaze.

"Still, even when we try to make regular improvements, all we receive is criticism. If only they were willing to understand us better," I said, slightly frustrated.

"Realize that those obsessed with criticizing and finding faults in others are actually your biggest allies, because they are the true supporters of your work, willing to spend time and effort identifying every mistake and shortcoming. Appreciate them for it. Be happy, my friend, because happiness isn't necessarily reserved for those who live in luxury; it belongs to those who live in simplicity and gratitude," said Kopral.

"But, if this weren't such a lonely path, we'd face less adversity," I said defensively, still unable to let go of the thought: '*Ah, if only...*'

"Don't complain about the difficulties that come your way, my friend. God doesn't send them to you; you are the one allowing them in. Remember, if you're still hesitant and fearful of doing good, you won't make any progress," Kopral said, his words resonating with me, stirring my thoughts and feelings.

Everything Kopral said was sobering. I had to grudgingly accept that he was right. Fantasizing about an ideal outcome, filled with 'if-onlys', could monopolize one's mind, leading one to expect perfection—even when perfection is unattainable. After all, perfection belongs only to the Creator, who holds the essence of Life.

When I snapped out of my reverie, I realized Kopral was nowhere to be found—he had already disappeared. My thoughts then turned to my mother, who had offered me advice when I didn't graduate on time. I struggled with writer's block while working on my final thesis and used the excuse of unfavorable circumstances to explain my lack of progress.

At the time, my mother simply said, "An artist who strives for perfection in everything often achieves nothing. If you wait until everything is perfect, you won't write a single word. So, get started. Write and find joy in the process. Don't let the fear of the process overshadow your aspiration. You won't fail unless you stop trying." I also recall Aristotle saying something similar: "Pleasure in the work puts perfection in it."

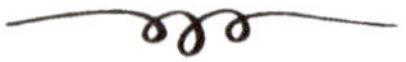

Working in the field of conservation, particularly in orangutan conservation, is never easy. The phrase 'if-only' is toxic, as it encourages waiting for ideal conditions before taking action. Dwelling on such wishful thinking in this line of work prevents us from tackling the ongoing challenges to protect nature. Therefore, it is crucial for everyone working to protect orangutans to build resilience in overcoming life's obstacles. Let's remain grateful in any situation and focus on the work at hand.

Fighters in any era do not rise to the challenge because everything is fine. History shows that champions were born in times of struggle, not in times of peace. Warriors emerge because the situation is dire. So, like those indomitable spirits, let us fight, take responsibility for our actions, and never give up. And let us always remember the words of Russian writer Leo Tolstoy, "If you seek perfection, you will never be satisfied."

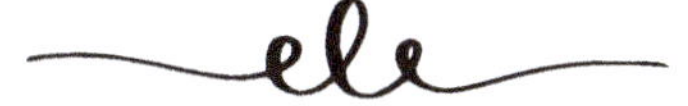

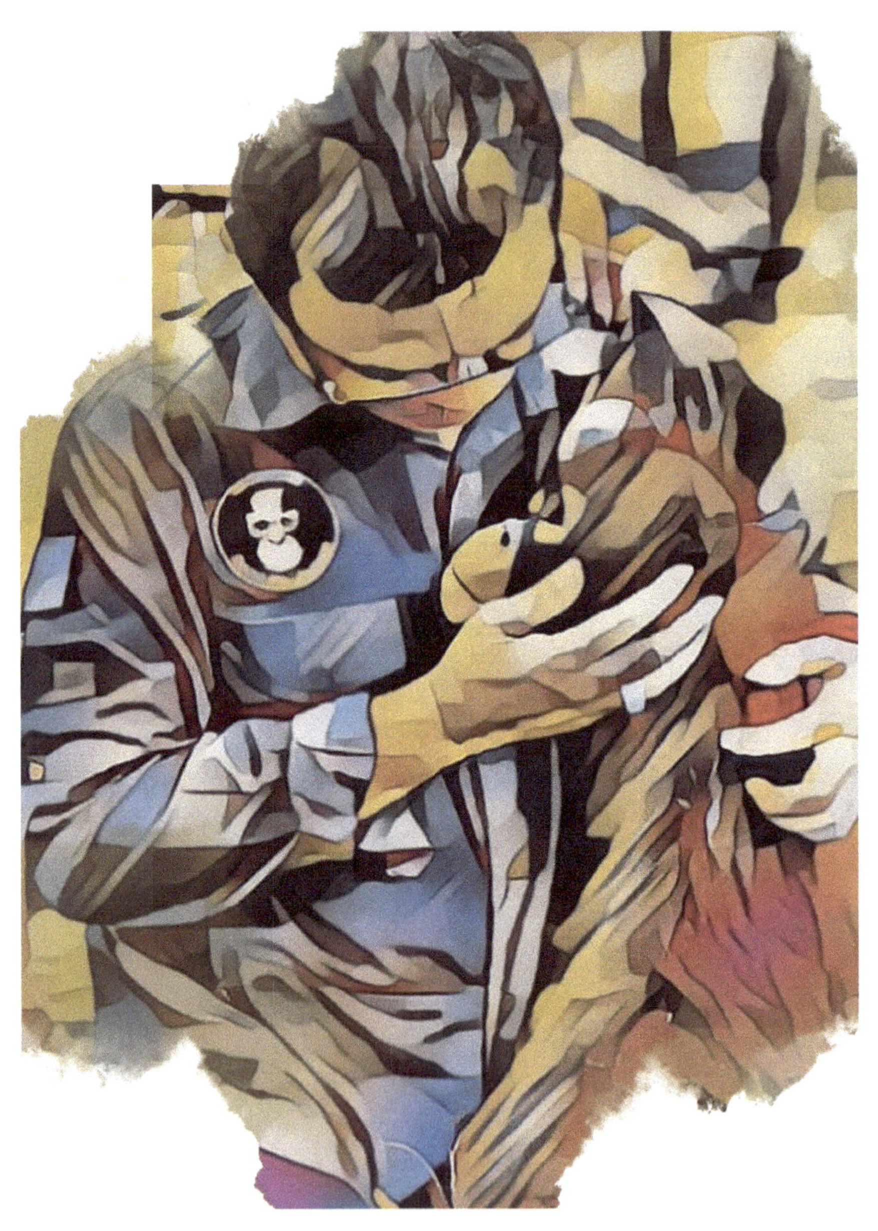

Fire can burn away trees,
And destroy forests,
But it can never extinguish
Our burning passion to help the orangutans

- JS in CNN 2015

Chapter 6

Walk Your Talk

One morning, after an exhausting and emotionally draining meeting, I decided to take a leisurely stroll through the forest of our orangutan rehabilitation center in Samboja Lestari, East Kalimantan. At that moment, I really needed to relieve the weariness in my mind, and I knew walking in fresh air, with its abundance of oxygen, would help calm the chaos I was feeling. As I breathed deeply, I wondered: *'What blessings from the forest have we taken for granted? What gifts and benefits have we failed to acknowledge or appreciate—never even pausing to consider the forest itself?'*

Walking on a slippery trail in the woods after the rain, I had to be extra cautious with every step. After 45 minutes, I sat on a fallen log, looking ahead where the trail led. Mentally, I was also "looking ahead"—focusing on the future, not the past.

While catching my breath, I looked around me. The only sight that greeted me was the charred remains of trees, blackened and reduced to charcoal. Remnants of plants that had once grown strong and tall were now silenced by the scorching blaze. The wildfire had indiscriminately claimed everything in its path.

I remember how much my colleagues and I at the Orangutan Foundation had poured our sweat and tears into caring for and protecting the forest. Looking further back, I could still recall the excitement and the hopeful pounding of my heart in the early days when I first joined the team working to develop the forest. I couldn't have been happier. After all, this forest had been created for the sole purpose of schooling orangutans uprooted from their natural habitat. It had taken us years to build, but now it had been completely ravaged in a matter of hours!

In the aftermath of the forest fire tragedy, I still vividly remember how we spent days cooling down the soil layers and conducting assessments to ensure no embers remained that could spark another fire. After all, it takes years to build a forest, but destroying it takes no time at all!

I was overwhelmed with bitterness and sadness when I heard the faint voice of Taymur, an adolescent male orangutan we repatriated from Kuwait. He softly spoke to me through my thoughts.

"Hello, my friend. Why are you so quiet? What's on your mind?"

"Look at the aftermath of the forest fire!" I said, my voice rising in anger. "We spent years planting these trees and nurturing them into a thriving forest, but now, they're gone in an instant. I can't believe how heartless and easy it is for others to cause such destruction. This loss makes me think of the blood, sweat, and tears we put into developing this forest, and it's leaving me feeling angry and devastated," I said, my chest tight with grief.

"Yes, it is indeed *that easy* for you humans to cause destruction, as easy and uncaring as when you take us from the arms of our mothers and sell us overseas. Yet, you do go to great lengths to bring us back, nurture us, and teach us the way of orangutans so that one day we can return to the wild," Taymur trailed off, reflecting thoughtfully. "But, just like one reckless word can jeopardize your kindness, a spark of flame can undo years of effort in building the forest."

"I'm not sure I fully understand what you mean, Taymur."

"Let me remind you that a tongue is like a fire that sets the whole forest ablaze. It is ferocious, unruly, and full of deadly poison. That's why there's a saying: 'One who guards his mouth preserves his life, but those who open their lips wide are doomed to perish,'" Taymur answered patiently.

"But that doesn't mean I can't get angry, right!?" I asked Taymur indignantly.

"No one is stopping you from being angry, my friend. Go ahead. Be furious. Even God gets enraged. But reflect on what Aristotle said: 'Anyone can be angry—that is easy. But to be angry with the right person, to the right degree, at the right time, for the right purpose, and in the right way—is not within everyone's power, and it's not easy,'" Taymur said simply, placating me.

"What you said is true," I conceded. "But whenever I remember the forest fire in Samboja, I feel disheartened. The once-mighty trees—full-grown plants—turned into charcoal in a matter of moments. Not to mention how some members of our team became exhausted and injured while trying to put out the fire. I don't understand why it's so hard for people to grasp that this forest is not just useless land to be burned or repurposed. In fact, humans have reaped many benefits from it," I said emphatically.

"So, tell me what happened when you were working to extinguish the fire close to the BOSF work area at that time?" asked Taymur curiously.

"Well, our experiences in Central Kalimantan were different from those in East Kalimantan. Each location posed its own challenges, so we also experienced different emotions at each one," I explained.

"Okay. So, tell me, my friend. I am ready to listen to your experience," he said.

"Alright," I agreed. In my mind, Taymur came closer and sat across from me, face to face. He was so close that I could see the reflection of my own eyes in his.

"So, the forest fire in our work area in East Kalimantan spread so quickly that it alarmed us. The dry season had made the bush extremely dry, turning it into easy fuel for the wildfire that consumed the trees we had planted decades ago. Despite our anxieties, we did our best to stay focused and manage the fire. We knew that if we couldn't control our emotions, the consequences would be dire."

"But, didn't I also hear that you had quite an incident because of poor judgment?" teased Taymur, smiling mischievously as though he knew a secret. Maybe he had encountered condescending humans who thought they were clever but were really just exposing their own flawed thinking.

"Wow, apparently, the leaves can't hide what we've done," I replied, feeling ashamed and keeping my eyes downcast.

"When the fire started, we sent our team to the hotspot to prevent it from spreading further. However, we forgot the possibility that the wind might carry stray embers—small flecks of burning debris—that could ignite dried, flammable leaves or twigs and start spot fires anywhere. While the team was focused on putting out the main fire, we suddenly received news of a new fire near the road leading towards our office, which meant it was approaching the orangutan enclosures. We had no choice but to mobilize everyone at the office to deal with this new fire. That was our only option.

With whatever tools we had, we rushed to the source of the fire and did our best to put out the flames. But, since we weren't equipped with proper safety gear, I ended up getting injured. None of us were wearing the special firefighting goggles needed for protection, and I was only wearing my everyday glasses. As a result, a small shard of charcoal, carried by the wind, lodged in my eye. Every time I blinked, the fragment scratched the surface of my eye. It was incredibly painful. Long story short, when I returned to Jakarta, I had to see an ophthalmologist for treatment. That was just one part of the story—my eye injury.

Then there was the experience of fighting the fire itself. The heat of the fire had raised the air temperature to unbearable levels. We were so focused on splashing water on ourselves to cool down that we forgot the shoes we were wearing were constantly stepping on burning embers, which caused the soles to melt. As a result, our feet were burned by the intense heat, adding another layer of misery to our ordeal," I told him with a sigh.

"Considering what happened, I'm reminded of a Swahili proverb, 'Running doesn't mean you'll arrive at your destination.' Although you and your team acted quickly, you didn't approach the situation tactically," Taymur responded.

"That was the tale of poor judgement that you asked about earlier," I said. After a pause, I added somberly, "In hindsight, we should have thought ahead and taken more preventive measures. For example, we could have bought affordable swimming goggles as alternative eye protection as a backup for the special firefighting goggles. Instead, I ended up spending a small fortune to treat my injury at the eye specialist. Well, I guess that was the price I had to pay for learning the lessons."

"On another note, why did you say that we didn't think tactically?" I asked, genuinely curious.

"Look, whenever you do anything, you're bound to encounter difficulties and make mistakes. Wanting to avoid them is natural—it's very human. But, I encourage you not to give up halfway through. It's precisely in those moments that you learn from your mistakes to improve.

As the Chinese saying goes: '*Fēngbào shǐ shùmù shēnshēn zhāgēn*'—storms make trees grow stronger and develop deeper roots. So in your case, when planning for future fires, you must prioritize what needs to be protected. In the event of a fire, get a drone in the air to monitor the area. If the fire is far from the orangutan enclosures, there's no need to deploy all your resources there. This is why I said you weren't making sound tactical decisions. Remember you can't do everything at once. You must have a priority. As Confucius said, 'He who chases two rabbits, catches neither.'"

"Thank you for your advice and insight," I replied to Taymur.

"So, you must have been under a lot of pressure at the time," Taymur asked, his face serious.

"The incident was terrifying. I was so stressed I felt as if my head was about to explode. Imagine—a new fire igniting less than 100 meters away from the orangutan enclosures in a forest we had planted 15 years ago! How could I not be stressed?! And on top of that, I was still dealing with the aftermath of that injury because of my lack of experience in handling the situation!" I exclaimed, agitated.

Then, in a calm, wise tone, Taymur responded, "Have you ever considered the words of the ancient Greek philosopher Epictetus? He said, 'Happiness and freedom begin with a clear understanding of one principle: what is within our control and what is not.' Now, tell me about your experience in Mawas, Central Kalimantan?"

"The forest and land fires in Central Kalimantan didn't just create thick haze but also threatened the lives of all the forest-dwelling wildlife. During the fire in September 2015, our team, in collaboration with the Central Kalimantan BKSDA (Balai Konservasi Sumber Daya Alam—Natural

Resource Conservation Center), managed to rescue two orangutans trapped by the flames within a week. Our team also saved a poor baby orangutan who was emaciated, weak, and malnourished. As a result of all of this indiscriminate burning of forest and land, it wasn't just humans who suffered the consequences—wild animals, such as the orangutans, also lost their homes, and in some cases, even their lives!" I explained to Taymur hotly, my chest tightening as the memory rushed back to me.

"Didn't the BOSF team also rescue orangutans in the Mawas area—the site that was once part of the Mega Rice Project (rice granary)?" Taymur asked urgently.

"Hold on, Taymur. Let me catch my breath," I said, trying to regulate my breathing. After a moment, I explained, "Sorry. Even though there's no smoke around us, just recalling the rescue mission is so distressing that it's making it hard to breathe."

Then, I began my story, "That rescue mission was to save a group of orangutans stranded along the banks of Mangkutub River in Kapuas regency, Central Kalimantan. It was a crucial mission because the area surrounding Mangkutub could no longer support the remaining orangutan population. The area had sustained extensive damage from massive forest fires and illegal logging, which accelerated the destruction of their habitat."

My mind wandered back to the 2015 forest fire. "It wasn't an easy rescue, as our efforts were hampered by a thick haze of smoke. The smoke clearly affected the health of both humans and orangutans. When the haze rolled in, dust particles and residual carbon from the flame entered our respiratory tracts, causing severe allergic reactions. These could lead to infections like bronchitis and pneumonia, due to a weakened immune system. But, despite the risks, we had no choice. Our team still had to rescue the orangutans," I explained to Taymur.

"At least you survived and managed to get out safely, even though you were almost lost in the smoke," he said with a faint smile.

I was surprised. How did Taymur know we had been stuck on a boat, lost for hours, with no idea where we were? At the time, not only did the dense smoke block our visibility, but our compass also stopped working. As a result, we were going in circles in the middle of the river, while slowly trying to navigate back to the riverbanks so we could follow them. I still get chills when I think about it. It was a really tense and stressful experience. But thanks to His Grace, we were able to return to our point of departure, though sadness and a sense of defeat enveloped us because we had failed to reach our destination.

"Dense fog and poor visibility were truly our main obstacles, hindering the rescue of individual orangutans trapped in the forest and land fires," I said faintly, almost mumbling.

"What else happened? Please continue with your story, my friend," Taymur asked.

"During the 2015 forest fire, which occurred between November and December, we managed to rescue 39 orangutans. We worked almost non-stop. Our efforts were slowed down at one point when the engine of the boat we were using exploded and was destroyed after being forced to run beyond its capacity. We had to stop the rescue operations close to Christmas because several members of our team were too exhausted, and some even had to be hospitalized.

After the New Year of 2016, between January and February, we resumed our rescue efforts, and as many as 37 orangutans were translocated to safer areas. But during the operation, we also found the carcass of one orangutan. Ah! If only we had more energy at the time, maybe that orangutan wouldn't have died. Alas, sometimes we have to accept that not everything we want can be achieved at once—especially considering how depleted our physical and mental energy was. That remains one of the saddest memories from the numerous rescue operations we've ever done." I concluded.

"You BOSF people are totally crazy!" Taymur cried suddenly. The outburst, a spontaneous expression of genuine emotion, reminded me of the words of Obelix, a character from the Asterix comics—which I often read to unwind after exhausting chemistry exams in my school days.

Then he continued, "We, orangutans, bear witness that there are still kindhearted humans who are willing to use their power for good. Although the journey is full of trials and tribulations, overall, the efforts to protect orangutans can be likened to a strong blind person lifting a sighted person who is blind to the truth. Think about it—many have heard, even seen, the forest and land fires, and know the impact these fires have on wildlife like us orangutans, but they stay silent!" Taymur said furiously. "Meanwhile, you," he continued, "despite the dense fog and smoke blocking your visibility, nothing stops you from taking action solely for the survival of us orangutans," he remarked.

Then Taymur, the orangutan we successfully repatriated from Kuwait, continued to express his opinions passionately, his voice filled with anger and tears in his eyes. "If only—yes, this is my utopian ideal, my friend—if only everyone was willing to make the effort and do what needed to be done, instead of just following the rules and sticking to the habit of inaction."

That was the last thing I remembered before he faded from my thoughts.

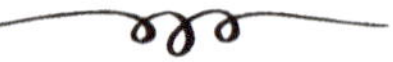

Don't get caught up in rhetoric. Rhetoric is "a tool for persuasion, aimed at believability, not an instruction on determining right from wrong," said Plato, the ancient Greek philosopher.

Once again, I gained profound insight from the orangutans' perspective through the tough experience of overcoming the forest fire in our conservation work area. Despite the disappointment, anger, and injuries, I'm glad that we didn't give up. Instead, we learned so much from those experiences, just as Aristotle said, "We cannot learn without pain."

Consider this: we will lose 100% of our chance to save orangutans if we never make any effort to do so. The opportunity to create change has been given to us all by our Creator. So take action now—otherwise, the changes we hope to see will never become reality!

'*Non est ad astra mollis e terris via*'—there is no easy way to reach the stars from the earth, as the Roman philosopher Seneca the Younger once said. Yes, that is indeed true, just as there is no easy way to save the orangutans from extinction. But we can do it, once we fully understand why we must act together!

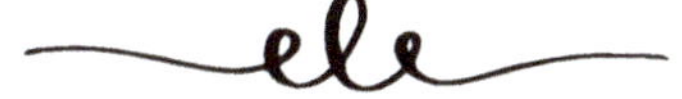

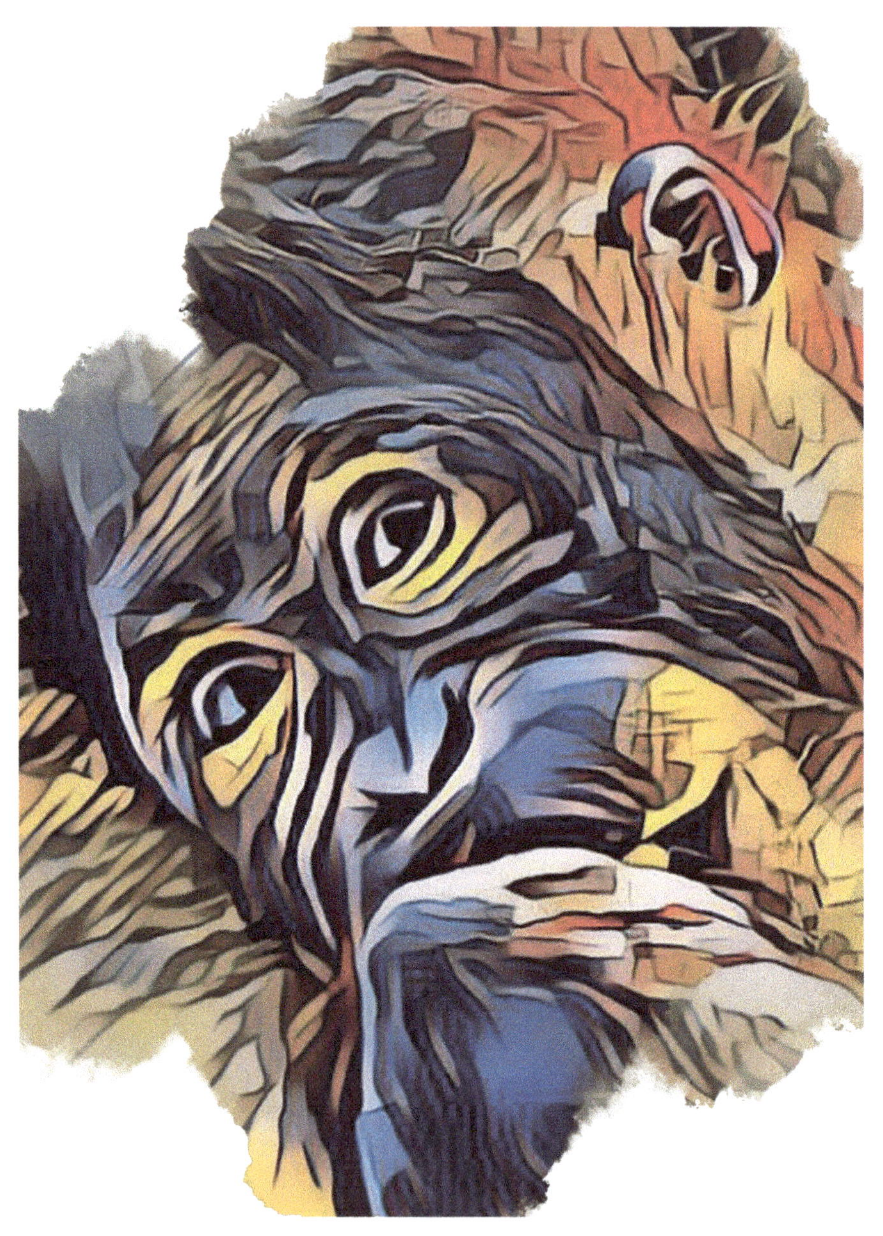

My child, the forest is a kingdom,
Where the altar wayfarers swear fealty lies,
Pledging to guard the land for life,
As a sacred vow of their devotion.

-RWW-

Orangutan Goes to School (OGTS)

The progress of a nation is often reflected in the education of its people, as education serves as one of the primary means of passing down customs, habits, skills, and knowledge from one generation to the next.

Today, character education has become a major focus for many nations. It is a deliberate, well-planned effort, implemented through learning environments to foster the development of human potential in future generations. Its aim is to shape a society with strong character, good moral conduct, and ethical values, so that individuals' choices and actions have a positive and constructive impact on nature and society.

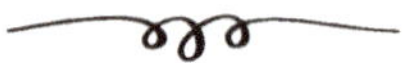

One day, after a long journey across peatland under the scorching sun, we arrived at the orangutan release camp in the Mawas area—a peat swamp forest that was once part of the planned million-hectare Mega Rice Project. The clean water in the peatland, though the color of Coca-Cola, was still clear enough to use as a mirror, reflecting the beauty of the sky without us having to raise our heads. Looking at the sky reminded me of watching my orangutan friends at Forest School, always climbing the tall trees and making my neck ache. Despite the soreness, I took pleasure in observing them play in the treetops while enjoying the ever-changing sky.

That day, I remembered my friend Davi, a female orangutan from the Forest School in Samboja Lestari, East Kalimantan. The moment I thought of her, my mind connected with hers, and we had a lively, imaginary chat. In my mind's eye, I saw Davi persistently tugging at her friend's arm—in an invitation to play while exploring the treetops.

"Davi, why do you keep pulling your friend's arm?" I asked.

"I'm trying to encourage him to play and relearn how to be a true orangutan," she said simply. "I need him to understand that we're meant to live in the trees, and we can't keep doing the things humans taught us when we were kept as pets. I'm the one reminding him of this, because we have similar backgrounds. Our pasts were shaped by humans who domesticated us. If we can't overcome the effects of domestication, then our skills and instincts as orangutans will slowly disappear. And I don't want that to happen. That's why I've been pulling my friend's hand, trying to get him to climb the tree," she explained.

"I realize that, even though at Forest School you're teaching us the ways of the forest so that our skills and abilities can reemerge, some still fail to learn," Davi said. Then she added indignantly, "And I don't want my best friend here to be one of them; I don't want him to not come back to the forest," she said sharply.

"But his learning doesn't have to be forced like that, Davi," I argued, defending the orangutan she kept pulling up.

But it seemed my words fell on deaf ears. She was still tugging at his hands, making a valiant attempt to get her friend to venture up to the treetops.

Then I heard Davi mutter under her breath, "You know, the roots of teaching and education may be bitter, but the fruit is sweet. Imam Shafi'i, an Arab theologian, once said, 'O young ones, if you cannot bear the fatigue of learning, you will have to endure the poignant bitterness of ignorance.' And we orangutans don't want to be ignorant," she said resolutely.

I gasped in surprise at Davi's words, realizing how true they were. What other lessons should I learn from this orangutan?

Davi spoke more firmly, "My friend, understand that we are in the current predicament because humans have not properly taught your generation how to love and respect nature. Loving us orangutans doesn't mean uprooting us from our habitat and placing us in human homes. That is a profoundly dangerous mistake. The current education only sharpens your logic, but it does not educate your hearts."

"I don't understand what you mean, Davi. Can you please repeat what you just said?" I asked, curious.

"Most education systems around the world prioritize intelligence. To introduce new ideas and shape the character of the younger generation, you need to be part of the existing system and create new programs that contribute to this goal, right? Next, you must establish a framework for character education, ensuring that the available means of expression support the optimal development of the younger generation and help them become well-rounded individuals. This will help achieve the goal of shaping quality individuals—those who are caring, self-aware, considerate of others, and who possess strong moral character and principles."

Davi's statement made me frown.

"Well, to raise awareness about conservation and the environment, we have developed a youth outreach program called Orangutan Goes To School (OGTS). Don't worry, it's not the orangutans themselves coming to the schools; rather, we're bringing the knowledge and awareness about orangutans and their habitat to the schools. Through this program, we educate the younger generation about the importance of orangutans to human lives. This is the core of the OGTS concept."

I tried to explain to her that there's a growing movement in society to educate the younger generation about developing awareness, empathy, and ethical consideration in respecting nature.

"That's a great step, my friend. We're glad to hear about the movement. We orangutans have high hopes for the OGTS program. When running this program, remember to speak in a way your audience understands—especially when you're presenting your ideas—so that they can easily absorb the information. Communicating in their language will make it easier for them to connect with the important issues. As Aristotle, the Greek philosopher, once said, 'Educating the mind without educating the heart is no education at all,'" she said sagely.

Incredible! Once again, I learned something new from Davi, this clever orangutan.

Davi continued, "As part of educating the younger generation, you also need to emphasize that the beauty of nature is proof of the Creator's love for us. After all, we don't inherit the Earth from our ancestors; we borrow it from our children and grandchildren. So, at the very least, let's return what we've borrowed in the same condition."

"I agree with you, Davi. That's also the goal of our program. We want them to fully understand the reasoning behind caring for orangutans. Hopefully, these children will grow up to be the ones making decisions in our society. We hope the knowledge we impart—through ongoing OGTS programs—about the importance of orangutans and their habitat will be deeply ingrained in their memories," I replied.

"Yes, absolutely! Let's not become like the Greek philosophers who were ridiculed by the Romans with the saying: *'Barba crescit, caput nescit'*—'The beard grows, but the head does not grow wiser.' Hahaha," she laughed heartily. She then continued, "Hopefully, having benefited from the OGTS program, the next generation will be wiser in managing nature. Remember, a stone doesn't get a hole because of some immense force that hollows it out, but through the repeated drips of water that wear it down. Similarly, humans don't become wise after just one or two lessons, but through gaining insight over and over again. Consistency is key here," she explained wisely.

"Indeed, Davi. That's how my father taught me to study. Even a dull blade can become sharp if it's constantly sharpened, and learning is the same. In learning, 10 x 2 is far better than 2 x 10. So thank you for encouraging us not to abandon character education. As Einstein said, 'The true sign of intelligence is not knowledge but imagination,'" I said, looking down, feeling insignificant compared to this intelligent orangutan. Conversing with Davi even made me think of Einstein—the physicist famous for his theory of relativity and quantum mechanics—which have since become the foundation of modern physics.

Then, Davi slowly disappeared, but I could still hear her voice shouting from afar: "Education is not as simple as eating chilies. It requires determination and persistence. Just like climbing a mountain, the stunning view comes after a tiring hike. So, don't be afraid of being different; be afraid of being the same as everyone else."

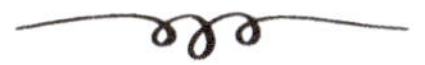

'Solum nati sumus non nobis'—We are not born for ourselves alone, said the Roman philosopher Marcus Tullius Cicero. As long as we are alive, we hope that future generations will care more about orangutans. Through the OGTS program, we hope that educated young people will gain awareness, become more compassionate, and develop the heart to understand that they are neither too lofty nor too smart to join the conservation movement—a movement filled with sweat, tears, and surprises.

If these younger generations believe that those working in the forest with orangutans are simple people without higher aspirations, then the character-building program may have missed the mark and may as well not be offered. Whenever these young people judge others solely by appearances, they miss the opportunity to meet some truly remarkable and inspiring individuals.

Let us not be quick to feel proud of what we've accomplished today, for we can never know what tomorrow will bring. Remember that knowledge and wisdom can be acquired by observing nature. Seeking knowledge is *taqwa* (piety)—devotion to the Creator; conveying and sharing knowledge is *ibadah* (worship)—an act of service to the Creator; and repeating knowledge is *dhikr* (remembrance)—a recitation as an act of remembrance. Seeking knowledge is a *jihad* (striving for self-improvement), said Abu Hamid al-Ghazali.

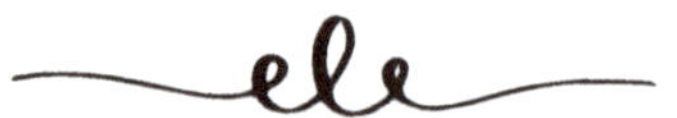

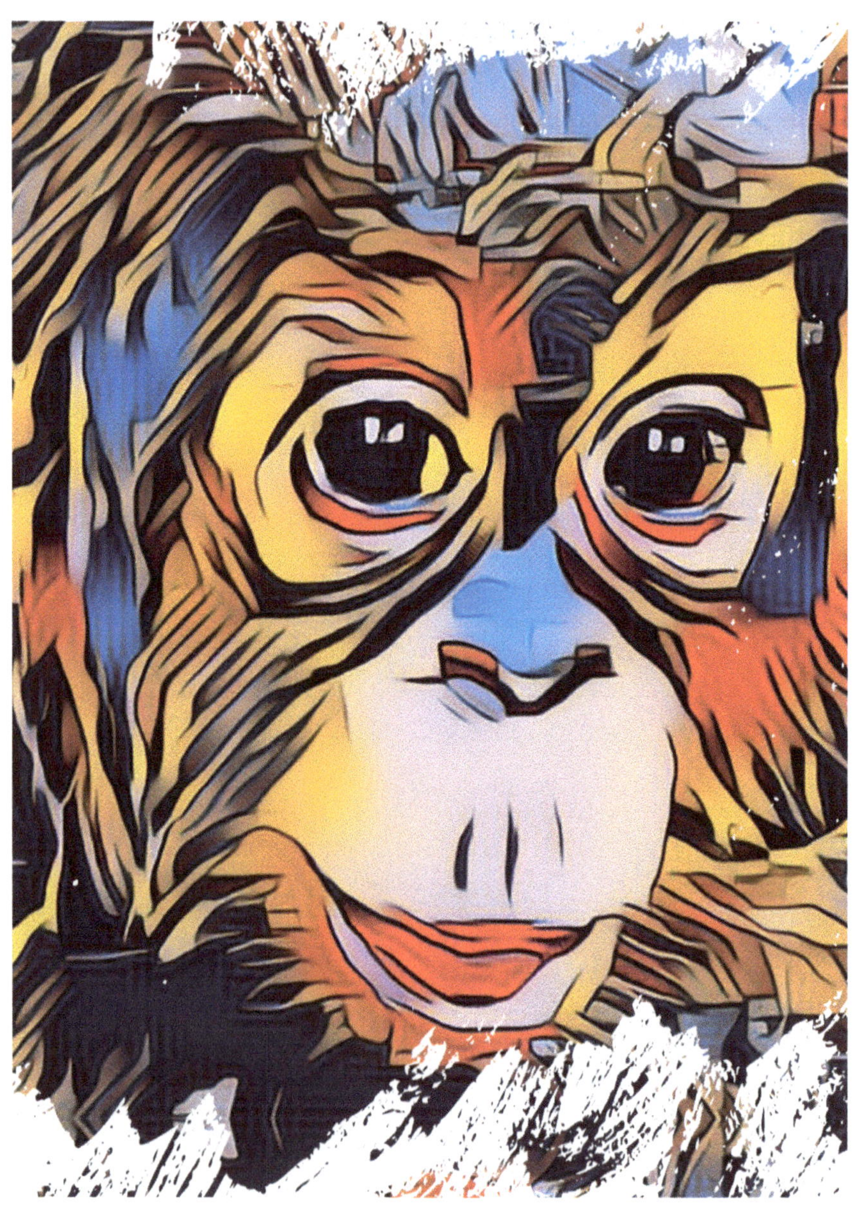

"Even bitter flavors can be savored"

Chapter 8

Return to True Nature

On release days, the exhaustion we feel from carrying out the release process fades the moment we see the orangutans roaming freely in the forest, where they truly belong. But does that mean our work is done? Is our job complete? Of course not. Once the cage is opened, monitoring begins.

The Post-Release Monitoring (PRM) phase is carried out to ensure that the freed orangutans are safe and able to survive in the wild. Monitoring is a physically demanding job that requires stamina. Climbing up and down hills to track and record the orangutans' activities in the forest becomes part of the daily routine for the monitoring team and their companions.

One afternoon, after a release, as the orangutans sat down to rest, it was time for the monitoring team to take a break as well. While we were relaxing by the bank of a crystal-clear river, we unpacked our food supplies and recharged after a long morning of work. The cool, fresh air and the clean water made any food provided by the monitoring camp taste like a feast. It's true what our elders say: the best cook in the world is a hungry stomach.

While enjoying my meal, my gaze swept across the surroundings until it eventually settled on the tall trees with swaying branches. There, I noticed the movement of an orangutan approaching the team, who were on their lunch break. When the orangutan drew closer—close enough for us to make eye contact—I realized I was looking at Suayap. Suayap was a female orangutan, repatriated from Thailand and rehabilitated at BOSF's (Borneo Orangutan Survival Foundation) Nyaru Menteng Rehabilitation Center in Central Kalimantan. It had taken her more than 16 years to finally return to her true home—the forest.

"Hello, Suayap, have you eaten yet?" I greeted her. "Or did you miss human food so much that you came to join us on our lunch break?" I continued, smiling teasingly at her.

"Hahaha, you simply can't tempt me, my friend. Even though my friends and I were once taught—and even forced—to live like humans, we are still orangutans. Then, at Forest School, you taught us how to become true orangutans, introduced us to the foods that are natural for us, and gave us the skills to defend ourselves when necessary. We were taught to actively explore our environment, to be skilled at foraging for natural foods, and to act appropriately in any situation. And now you're tempting me to eat human food? Do you want me to go back to being misguided as we were before, because of human conditioning?" Her voice rose in indignation.

I recoiled in surprise at her response. I couldn't fathom why she was so upset. Was it a result of my teasing, her stress, or perhaps a combination of both? My mind raced through all the possible reasons, and I suddenly realized I had stopped eating without even noticing.

"Why the silence, my friend? Come on now, let's not be too sensitive," she chided, smiling.

"I'm just soaking in the atmosphere," I replied with a huff, deflecting her astute (and accurate) inference. Maybe I had been too caught up in my feelings. "Anyway, what message brought you here to tell me, instead of exploring the forest, Suayap? Shouldn't you be enjoying your freedom?" I added, trying to sound friendlier.

"Thank you for bringing us home to the forest, to our *fitrah* as the Indonesians say—the essence of our creation," she said.

Before she continued, I asked, "So what is your understanding of freedom now that you've returned to your home in the forest?"

She sighed. "Although freedom has been our dream ever since we were domesticated by humans, it's not the be-all and end-all for us orangutans. We don't idolize freedom. It's true that living without freedom is like living without a soul. But, in the back of our minds, we know that worshiping freedom is like a fish desiring freedom, but living on land.

Not only is such a life no longer beneficial, but, in fact, it is harmful. Freedom doesn't imply living without control; rather, it's about exercising self-restraint so you can do what you want without jeopardizing the safety of others," she responded, gazing intently into my eyes.

"Ah, you're making me feel ignorant, my friend," I quipped, resuming my lunch. I realized her answer had successfully provoked me, leaving my mind in a whirlwind of thoughts. To mask my discomfort, I asked, "Suayap, aren't you afraid of being alone and helpless in such a vast forest? After all, you were used to living on a small island sanctuary where food was always provided for you," I babbled, trying to deflect my dumbfoundedness after hearing her thoughts on freedom with a ridiculous comment.

"Don't be so hard on yourself, my friend. We orangutans were created and placed in the forest by God, the Owner of Life. Now that we've returned to our *fitrah—* our natural state—in the habitat that suits our nature, nature itself has become our greatest teacher," she said, smiling serenely. "After all, God gave us one tongue but two ears, so we can listen twice as much as we speak. Similarly, this will also help humans learn—although, as the Greek philosopher Heraclitus once said, 'Much learning does not teach understanding,'" she added, philosophically.

"By the way, where did you learn about Greek philosophers, my friend? Didn't you get most of your education from my colleagues?" I teased her with a smile. I admired her ability to harness and learn from the essence of nature to gain wisdom. Perhaps this newfound insight reflected her happiness now that she was free in the forest, just as Plato once said, "Justice, truth, and freedom are at the root of happiness."

Then, suddenly Suayap veered off on a tangent. "Since you're accustomed to drinking black coffee, you know that brewing it is an art. Pouring hot water into a cup is like pouring out the feelings in your heart. In that way, coffee may be the best and the most understanding companion in difficult moments. It proves that enjoyment can be found even in bitterness."

I was blown away by Suayap's insightful analogy. Indeed, working in orangutan conservation often means confronting uncertainty and bitterness. At times, the work feels like trudging up a hill, and other times, it's like falling freely from the top. As a result, sadness, anger, and guilt become a symphony of emotions that must be accepted with gratitude.

"You know, my friend," she interrupted my racing thoughts again, "if jokes no longer make you laugh, and pain no longer makes you sad, then find happiness in solitude, with only God by your side," she said sagely. "The world belongs to those who dare to take risks, dare to be disappointed, and dare to be alone. When you returned us to our *fitrah*, our natural state, you never thought of yourselves as heroes, and that's exactly how it should be. Restoring our rights to life after being uprooted from where we were created is not an act of heroism, and you've proven it."

"Thank you, Suayap," I said. "Explore this forest to your heart's content; watch the horizon without bars before your eyes or walls behind your back. Study this forest and do what God always intended your forefathers to do when He created you in the forest—to benefit the earth."

After that orangutan release and my participation in post-release monitoring, I once again gained a deeper understanding of what freedom and independence truly mean. Freedom is the ability and willingness to fulfill the purpose for which God created us. To be free doesn't just mean being free of physical shackles—it also involves respecting and supporting the freedom of others.

Each of us, including the orangutans, has roles and responsibilities in life, and the orangutans have a clear, inherent awareness of their place in nature. Have you ever wondered why the Lord of Life granted us freedom and life itself? Have you ever considered whether life is more than just finding food, gaining popularity, achieving goals, getting married, or starting a family? Have you ever reflected on the deeper purpose your Creator may have for you? Have you taken the time to examine your life and ask if you're fulfilling your soul's true purpose as intended by your Creator?

The released orangutans are now free and have returned to their *fitrah*—their true nature. Now that they are in their natural habitat, their true home as wild orangutans, they are free to carry out God's command to support human life.

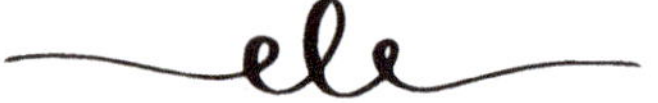

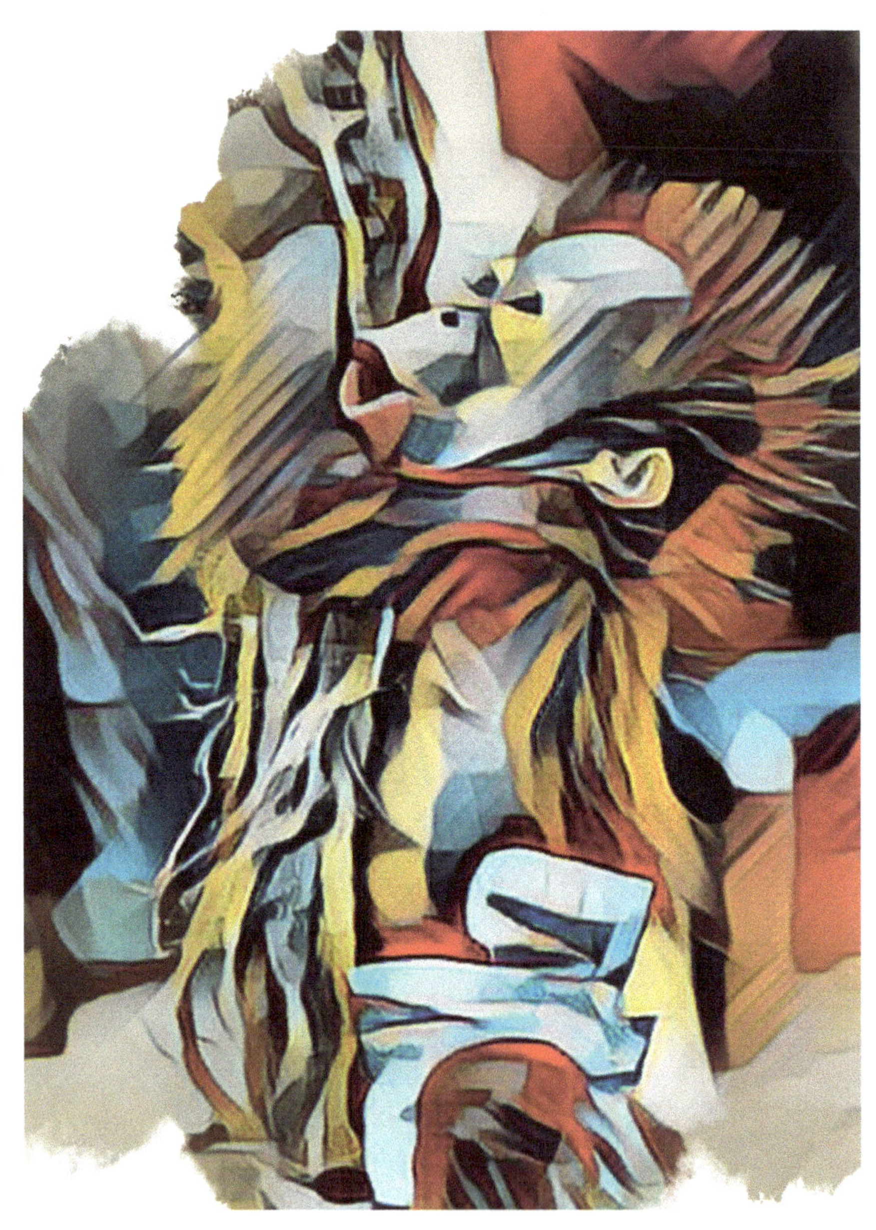

"A cage is no home for an orangutan,
They long for their true home, the forest."

Chapter 9

Homesick

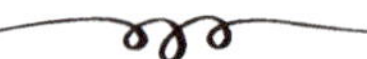

The COVID-19 virus has infected the entire global population, causing a pandemic. No country has been spared its effects. To mitigate the transmission of COVID-19, people have adopted social and physical distancing strategies, with many activities now taking place at home. Staying at home and limiting all social contacts and activities are expected to reduce the rapid spread of the virus from person to person.

So, the question becomes: Can we stay at home for weeks on end? Evidently, we cannot. Boredom eventually sparks a desire to defy the rules and rebel, sometimes even recklessly breaking them on purpose. Why does it happen? It seems that the monotony of being at home, even with our family, can breed boredom.

As the light faded one afternoon, amidst the boredom of being confined to my home, I found myself thinking about the orangutans at the BOSF (Borneo Orangutan Survival Foundation) rehabilitation center, who had spent years living in a 3x3x6 meter cage. I couldn't even begin to imagine how bored they must have been! The limited space within the cage and the iron bars surrounding it must have made them daydream and yearn for the forest that was once their home, even more. Some of these orangutans were kept in cages after contracting human-borne diseases. Many were displaced from their habitat and left with nowhere to live due to a few greedy humans who deliberately depleted the forest they called home. Others were admitted to the center for various reasons, all of which led to their confinement.

In the dimness of dusk, while quarantining at home to avoid contracting COVID-19, I thought of Cesar—one of my orangutan friends, who lived in a cage at the BOS Foundation's rehabilitation center in Nyaru Menteng, Central Kalimantan, Indonesia. Our minds connected and I found myself conversing with him.

"Hello, my friend!" exclaimed Cesar, the orangutan who could no longer be released into the wild due to his massive size and long captivity, which had rendered him unable to survive in the forest without human intervention. "You seem troubled. What's weighing on your mind?"

"Hahaha, it's actually you and your friends who are being confined that are making me upset," I replied, forcing a smile.

"Oh, how interesting! Do you want to tell me why?" he said, sitting down and looking intently into my eyes.

"What enables you to endure years of living in a cage?" I asked. Then, with a note of exasperation, I added, "It's only been one or two months since we've had to stay at home with only our family to interact with, yet we're already so bored that some of us have even started challenging the lockdown restrictions and leaving the house."

"That means you and your kind are experiencing a condition called *cabin fever*. You must have heard of it, haven't you?" he said.

I was too embarrassed to admit I hadn't, but he continued before I could reply. "*Cabin fever* describes the feelings of misery and restlessness that can occur when someone is isolated or confined indoors—be it at home or any other specific place—for a prolonged period of time. Being cut off from the outside world can also contribute to this condition. Symptoms include anxiety, decreased motivation, irritability, hopelessness, apathy, impatience, and depression. During this COVID-19 pandemic, you humans need to be more cautious about cabin fever, as many of you are house-bound for an indefinite period to reduce the risk of contracting the virus and prevent its spread. However, now you can better understand what it's like for us orangutans to live in isolation in cages for years."

"Wow, you impress me, Cesar. I have never heard of the term *cabin fever,* and here you are, explaining it perfectly," I said in amazement.

"'The more you read, the more you think; the more you learn, the more you realize you know nothing.' That's what Voltaire once said," he commented.

"Thank you for not mocking me for not knowing so much, Cesar," I replied, feeling a little embarrassed.

He then continued. "Don't let our aggressive behavior in our cages make you afraid to release us into the wild. What we're showing are signs of boredom because we miss our home in the forest. So come on, find a way to return us to nature," he said, his voice soft but firm, carrying an authoritative tone.

"If you humans get bored at home and start acting out due to the stress of pandemic restrictions, then you understand our predicament. We've been confined in cages for years, and I don't believe our feelings are all that different," he commented. "And realize that what we're truly missing is our home in the forest. Humans may be sick of their homes, but we are homesick," he lamented.

"I was angry when you humans forced me and my friends to leave our home in the forest. We were then forced to make peace with our new lives in cages, despite the fact that we yearn to be back among the dense foliage. Just so you know, those visions fuel the daydreams and desires that run through our minds, every day and every night."

"Yes, we truly understand how much you miss your home in the forest," I said to him carefully, not wanting to ruin the moment. The longing in his voice broke my heart.

"Home is where our life story begins. Home is where our life journey starts. Home is where we long to gather," he murmured. "For us orangutans, homesickness is not only the longing for a place to call home, but also our yearning for family and freedom, as God intended. So, please understand, home is more than just a place for us to return to. When we enter our home, all our memories come to life vividly. It may not be in the form of a grand building, but our home holds a treasure trove of priceless stories," he finished his explanation softly.

What Cesar said struck a chord with me. Of course, the orangutans are feeling homesick for their home in the forest. And this longing only intensifies, with no way for them to ease it, especially since they've also endured years of cabin fever without reprieve. His explanation echoed in my mind, bringing me to a deeper level of understanding of what the orangutans endured.

While humans were home-bound due to the COVID-19 pandemic, even when surrounded by their families, they may develop cabin fever from the isolation. Meanwhile, in the cages of the BOSF rehabilitation center, hundreds of orangutans like Cesar have suffered from cabin fever for years—some even for decades. These orangutans have also been forced to come to terms with their homesickness for decades. Yet so few humans in the world are aware of how much anguish the orangutans endure in captivity and in being unable to return home.

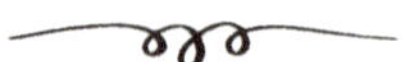

That day, I gained a new insight from the orangutans. I realized how much Cesar, the orangutan, respected his fellow creatures, by the way he imparted knowledge without making me feel ashamed of my ignorance. He kindly showed me that when offering advice, suggestions, or even criticism to someone in the wrong or ignorant about a topic, the message is better received when delivered in a gentle manner. This way, the recipient doesn't feel exposed and humiliated.

I was also struck by his understanding of the current human predicament due to isolation and how it mirrors what the orangutans have been enduring for years. While many people around the world experienced the emotional challenges caused by cabin fever, any aggressive or impatient behavior, regardless of the cause, is never justified or excusable.

The orangutan said, 'Do your work wholeheartedly. If you are disappointed, the worst thing you can experience is heartbreak, not a mental breakdown.' So, let us learn from the orangutans, who, despite being trapped in cages due to human actions, manage to maintain their emotional and mental well-being—even after years of not understanding why they have been subjected to such an experience. I recognize, however, that this is not easy to achieve.

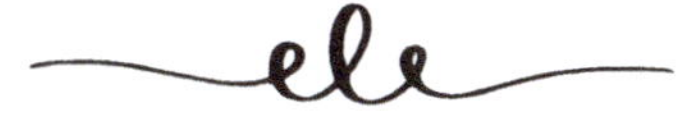

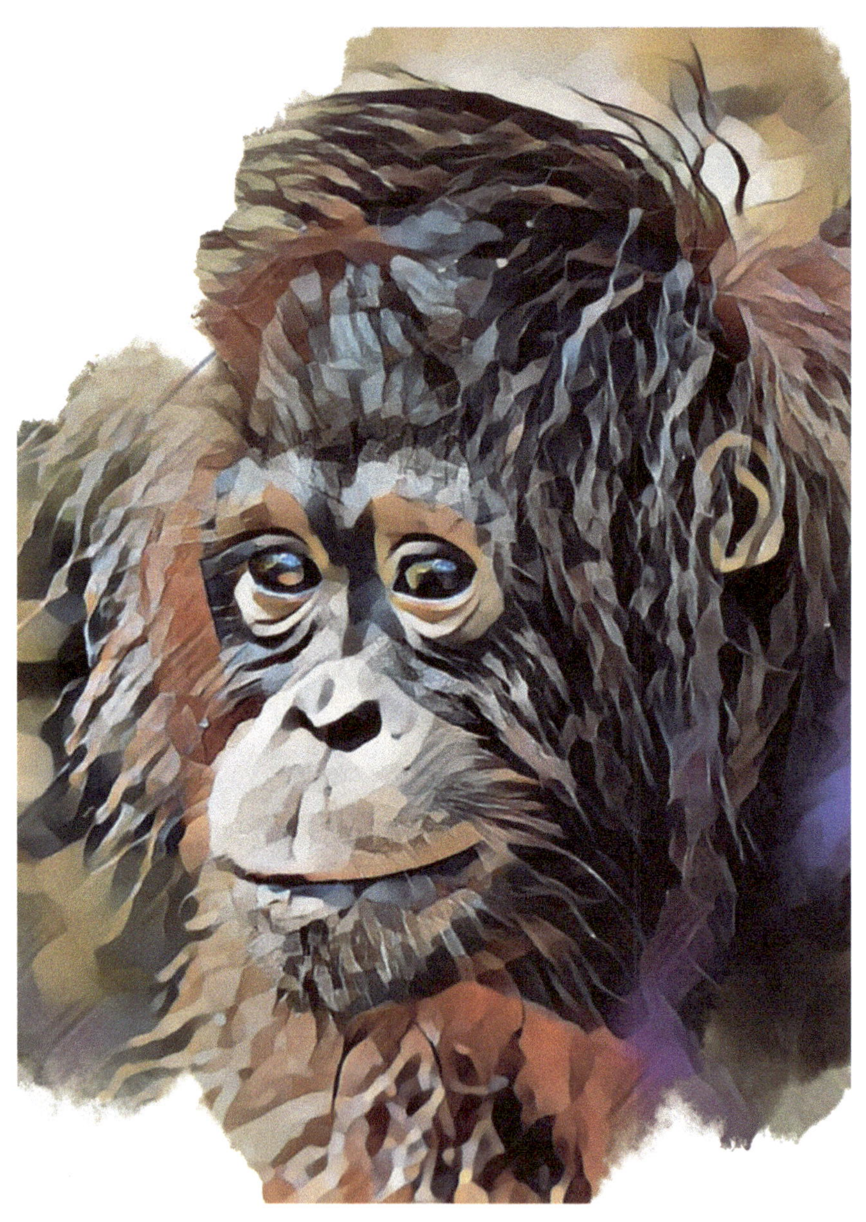

"Therefore, take care of yourself,
And protect all those in your care."

Chapter 10

Be a Conductor

After releasing an orangutan in the forest, I sat on a riverbank, appreciating the lush, verdant surroundings, and listening to the gentle gurgling of the river. It was a moment I truly savored. Being away from the hustle and bustle of the capital city and the constant barrage of hoaxes on social media felt like a true luxury. As I reflected on these gifts of life, while relaxing to the harmonious blend of an orchestra playing classical music and the sounds of nature, I couldn't help but wonder: *'What blessings from God had we taken for granted? What privileges had we failed to appreciate?'*

While savoring the beautifully evocative *Symphony No. 9* by Beethoven, performed by the Chicago Symphony Orchestra, I was startled by the splatter of water from a stone thrown into the river in front of me. I scanned my surroundings to see who had thrown the stone and disrupted my enjoyment. Looking up, I found an orangutan smiling at me from a branch of a large, lush tree. Sitting across from him, however, all I felt was irritation at the interruption.

"Why are you frowning and looking so annoyed?" the orangutan asked in a friendly tone.

"You're ruining my enjoyment of Beethoven's symphony playing on my phone," I snapped, feeling irritated. In the forest, a mobile phone served as nothing more than an ordinary music player.

"Why do you enjoy listening to the orchestra?" my new orangutan friend asked curiously. "Do you gain philosophical insights by listening to the symphony, especially in relation to conservation work or working with orangutans?"

"Of course. I suppose my colleagues and I at BOSF (Borneo Orangutan Survival Foundation) really work for you orangutans. You are our boss," I replied with a laugh.

"But, why orchestra, specifically?" the orangutan asked, his curiosity evident. He must have already known the answer, I thought, since I had always learned so much from them, from the orangutans.

"BOSF is a remarkable organization with highly skilled personnel," I replied. "Managing a team of such exceptional individuals is not easy. This is why an orchestra, which operates with a similar dynamic, can serve as a great model. Conservation work requires teamwork—a collective effort— where, within the team, no one individual is better than the others. Only in an orchestra can we truly see the power of teamwork, where all the members, along with the conductor, enjoy the camaraderie of working together, without any individual or group ego getting in the way. When have you ever heard of a pianist in an orchestra claiming to be better than a violinist, or vice versa? This is the essence of teamwork:

there is no "I" or "her" in a team. Just like a chain, we are all interconnected, and we support the weakest link. As a result, the orchestra maintains harmony and continuously creates a beautiful melody, right?" I explained.

"So, are you a commander or a boss?" asked the orangutan.

"In the past, a leader was considered a boss. But now, leaders need to be partners with those they lead. They can no longer lead solely based on structural power. Today's team is more like an orchestra, so I would say I am more like a conductor," I replied.

"So, would it be accurate to say that there is a difference between a boss and a leader?" my friend inquired. His tone was free of any challenge, only curiosity. "A boss would say, 'Do this,' whereas a leader would say, 'Let's do this together,' just like in an orchestra. Is that right?" he asked, then thoughtfully answered his own question.

"The philosophy and analogy you used are interesting, my friend," I said with admiration. "We can also see this reflected in the universe. Everything in nature affects everything else; nothing exists in isolation. A change in one place ripples through and affects life in other parts of the world. So, don't underestimate the impact of your actions on this earth. Every human thought influences life and the biodiversity in this world. This is the reality we observe in the universe. A human thought, no matter how small or seemingly insignificant, is like a note on the musical score of a symphony played by an orchestra. If the conductor fails to focus on the tempo, for example, a misstep will disrupt the entire rhythm. Similarly, if a violinist disregards the dynamics in the musical notation just to stand out, the harmony of the orchestra's performance will be compromised."

My orangutan friend became thoughtful, and then said, "That sense of togetherness is what needs to be fostered in a team. I remember a story carried by the wind about a South African philosophy that is similar to the symphony and orchestra concept you mentioned."

"Wow, apparently even you, in the jungle of Borneo, know about South Africa. My knowledge is nowhere near yours," I replied in amazement.

"As you explained earlier, everything is interconnected. The night breeze whispered to us about this philosophy at bedtime. It's called *Ubuntu*. It's an unusual and rarely heard word, right? Ubuntu is an African wisdom that means 'I exist because we exist.' How can someone be happy when another member of the family is suffering? Ubuntu is a term in the Nguni Bantu languages in South Africa, and it translates to 'Humanity towards Others.' Its philosophy speaks to the 'universal interdependence that links humanity'. This concept was adopted by post-apartheid South Africa as a tool to foster harmony and cooperation among many ethnic groups. At the heart of this concept is cooperation and togetherness," concluded the wise orangutan.

"I heard about this story from my mother when I asked her about family togetherness. She didn't specifically mention Ubuntu, but she did talk about the beautiful philosophy shared among the Zulu and other African tribes," I added, sharing the information with him.

"I'm curious to hear your mother's story. Tell me!" said my friend eagerly, like a child with a new toy. He might even share this story with his friends later. I was reminded of my father's words about knowledge. He once said, "If you have two oranges and give both to a friend, you'll have no more oranges left. But, if you have two pieces of information or knowledge and you share them with someone, you don't lose that knowledge."

"So, an anthropologist and researcher visited an area in South Africa and brought with him a basket full of fruit. Seeing a crowd, he said to the people, 'Come on, first come, first served—whoever is fastest gets all the fruit in the basket.' Do you know what happened? They all held hands and walked together to get the fruit, then divided it equally among themselves. The researcher asked, 'Why didn't you compete to take all the fruit for yourself?' They replied, 'We are all family; how can one of us enjoy the fruit when our brothers are sad because they get nothing?' Just like the body, when one hand is injured, the whole body feels it," I said, ending my mother's story.

"Exactly. This philosophy should be applied universally, especially in teamwork. A conductor may have more experience and a better understanding of each member of the team because he has been in their position. It's worth considering Immanuel Kant's words: 'Experience without theory is blind, but theory without experience is mere intellectual play.' Conservation work requires more than just intelligence; it also involves the management and art of harmonizing scientific knowledge with an understanding of the power of nature, all guided by the heart," said the orangutan, as he moved to a higher branch in the forest.

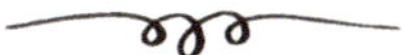

I became contemplative. I unexpectedly learned about teamwork from an orangutan. To be precise, he and I exchanged ideas that helped us realize that everything in this world is interconnected. The key, we concluded, is to build harmony together, just like in an orchestra.

Together, we become stronger. Even if we can't change everything, we can still contribute through small, simple actions. It is important to note that a small or simple action does not mean it is insignificant when creating change. Imagine if we constantly tried to change things beyond our control—it would be frustrating, hopeless, and even a waste of time, energy, and emotions.

Once again, our orangutan friend reminded us: "Let's work together as a team. Stay focused and remember to set your priorities, especially when it comes to the protection of orangutans and their habitat."

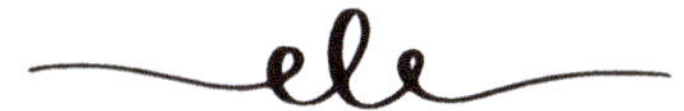

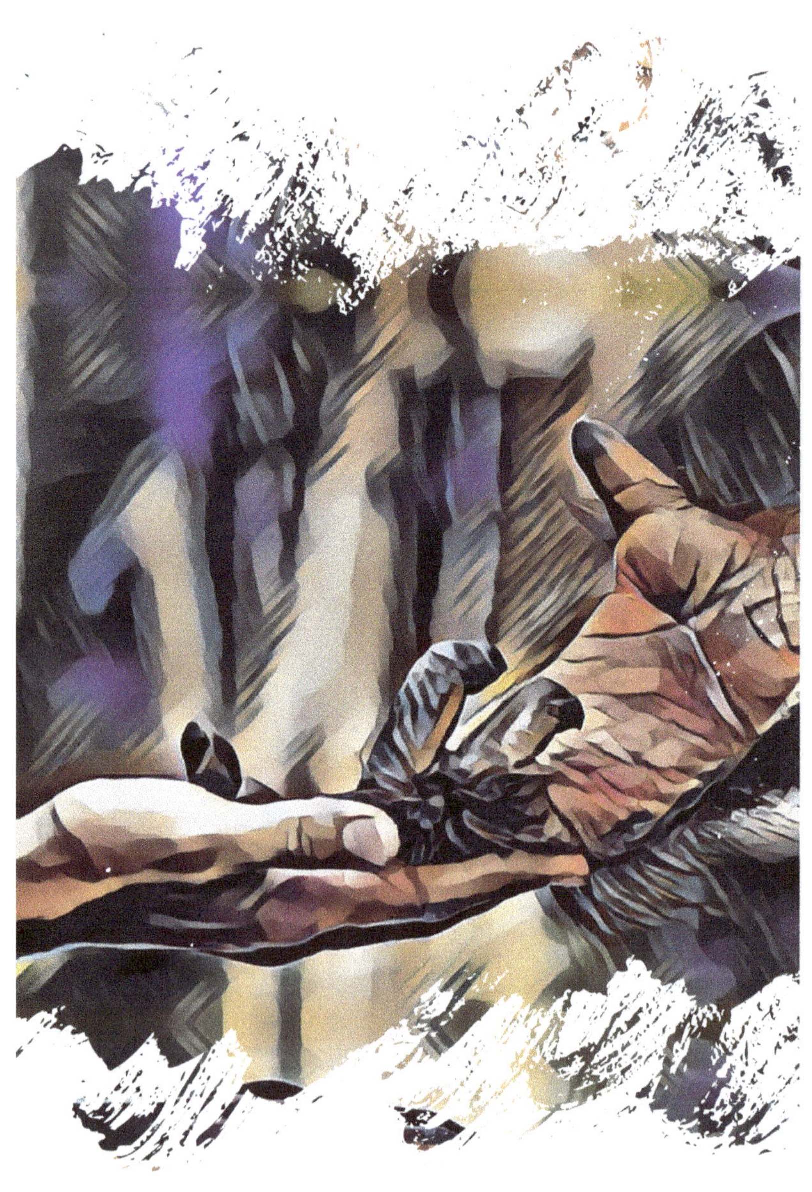

"Venter praecepta non audit' "

"A hungry belly will not listen to advice"

Chapter 11

Should Community Development be part of Conservation?

Once, I asked my father, "Why does the Church care for the poor? And why does the Church need deacons?" At the time, I was hoping he would give an in-depth answer filled with theological theories, as secretly, I enjoyed the back-and-forth of our debates. Even as a university student, I found myself more engrossed in reading philosophy and liberation theology than in my actual textbooks.

But my hope for a spirited discussion with my father was quickly dashed when, instead, he gave me a brief reply that took me by surprise. I was left speechless. That night, I lost myself in thoughts, mulling over his response.

He said: 'It is pointless to talk about God's goodness to those who are starving.' The Roman philosopher Seneca also echoed this sentiment with a saying in Latin: 'Venter praecepta non audit'—a hungry belly will not listen to advice.

Looking back, I realize that my father's words were not just relevant in that moment, but also to my work in natural resource conservation, even as I write this article today.

This kernel of wisdom can be translated as, 'Don't talk about conservation and the integrity of His creations while people are still starving.' This truth remains valid, even when efforts to safeguard the environment and preserve the integrity of creation face challenges posed by humanity's insatiable appetite and greed. While we may believe that God created a harmonious and abundant world for all His creations, as Gandhi wisely noted, that abundance is often not enough for two or three greedy individuals.

When we look at the activities of the Church, it's clear that its service often prioritizes the underprivileged. Yet, its efforts to uphold the integrity of creation tend to be less visible. In reality, there is ample evidence showing that marginalized communities frequently face ecological issues. Even on our way to the orangutan-release forests or conservation areas, we often pass through such lands suffering from environmental degradation.

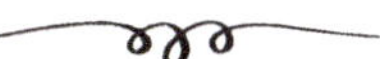

One night, during a torrential downpour, we found ourselves stranded deep in the interior of Kalimantan while on an orangutan release journey. Seeing the familiar sight of the damaged landscape through a new perspective was a jolt to my mind. Our vehicle was trapped in a mud pit, leaving us with nothing to do but make peace with nature. We had to wait until sunrise the next morning.

That evening, I sensed a pair of eyes on me, watching silently. It was an orangutan observing me from the shadows of the forest. Like my team and I, he was drenched by the rain. His gaze seemed to say, "It's okay for your body to be bathed in rain every once in a while. Just embrace nature's gift for the night." As our eyes locked on each other, a connection formed, and a silent dialogue began between us.

"Why are you anxious, my friend?" greeted the orangutan, whom I later came to know as Jacky.

"I'm stuck here tonight, wet and cold from the rain. Yes, I'm uncomfortable, but I can't help but think about how many people, because of poverty, endure for years what I'm experiencing right now. Where is the government's effort to help with the situation?" I replied, shivering with chattering teeth.

Instead of directly answering, Jacky said, "Martin Luther King once said, 'God never intended for one group of people to live in superfluous, inordinate wealth, while others live in abject, deadening poverty.'" He paused for a moment, then added, "But poverty isn't just an issue for the government. Clearly, poverty is a complex, deeply rooted social problem. Thus, the conservation movement has an important role to play in protecting and bringing about the integrity of God's creation, not just in nature, but also within communities. What these communities need is not just a lofty, idealistic program, but a genuine, active presence. They need initiatives with real, down-to-earth actions that create tangible impact."

"So, basically, you're saying that conservation work must work hand-in-hand with community development, right?" I asked my friend, Jacky the orangutan.

"Exactly. Conservation efforts should be part of the human liberation movement, especially for the poor and marginalized. This act of caring for others and offering service is an expression of love in action, just as He commanded, 'Love your neighbour as yourself.' Think about it—how can you claim to love us orangutans if you don't even care about your fellow humans?" Jacky challenged.

I was stunned. What he said forced me to rethink my previously established beliefs. The poor are also His creations, and there must be a purpose behind their presence among us. It became clear to me that conservation work isn't just about preserving nature, instead it's about glorifying God through maintaining the integrity of His creation. Therefore, if conservation efforts do not actively work to liberate the poor from poverty, how can we confidently claim to be safeguarding the integrity of His creation?

He interrupted my thoughts, "Why so quiet, my friend? It seems like your mind has drifted far away. Come back to reality and start thinking about how conservation and community development can align and work together," he said, gently coaxing me back to focus.

"Community development must be carefully planned and thoughtfully designed. Don't let obstacles or the fear of failure hold you back. There are two main reasons for failure: first, overthinking without taking action, second, ignoring the plan and skipping the necessary steps for implementation."

Jacky paused for a moment before continuing, "Economic progress and efforts to promote development and liberate people from poverty led to the idea—often driven by pity—that 'the hungry should be given fish.'

Then, there is the view that advocates for self reliance, which suggests that the less fortunate should be 'given fishing rods, instead of fish.' However, as society has progressed, simply providing fishing rods and other equipment is no longer enough. The fishing ponds are now controlled by those with capital, restricting access and creating structural barriers that perpetuate poverty.

That's why another perspective suggests a more sustainable solution: providing the poor with ponds and fish fingerlings (fish seed). This approach allows them not only to generate income, but also lift themselves out of poverty," he explained.

I was impressed. "In essence, community development should be based on the community's needs, so that the methods for building self-esteem and fostering independence can be tailored accordingly," I said, nodding in agreement. "Thank you for your insight, my friend."

I had to admit, Jacky had a remarkable understanding of the two goals to be achieved: community development and freedom from poverty. Perhaps being confined in a cage had allowed his mind to soar, and dream of freedom for so long. This gave him a fresh perspective, novel ideas, and an open mind. His insights were far more profound than anything I learned in development economics.

"When conservation work is mobilized synergistically with community development, the results will be remarkable. This partnership exemplifies the integrity of creation," he said. "This sense of empowerment will give those who are victims of an oppressive system power and control over their lives, enabling them to change their circumstances and escape poverty. It may not happen overnight, but with time and effort, it will. You do know that 'fast and easy' is just a slogan in advertising, right? Like the ads for instant noodles?" he joked. "Even then, don't you still have to wait for the water to boil before you can cook the noodles? So, think about it, where's the 'instant' in that process?" Jacky continued.

"I think I understand what you're saying, Jacky. Community development is about helping people gain the confidence to chart their own course in life. Its role is to liberate, not to give handouts out of pity," I said, summarizing my understanding to Jacky.

As Jacky the orangutan slowly moved away from me to find denser leaves for shelter from the rain, he said, "This is the role conservation work plays in promoting equality and fairness for all of creation, rather than merely invoking sympathy where the rich give the proverbial crumbs to the poor. This reflects the understanding and faith that God has come as the liberator of mankind, and we, who have been liberated, must also bring this freedom to others in creation."

With that, Jacky disappeared into the thick forest branches, heading to his home—the forest. "Thank you for liberating us and returning us to our habitat," he called out as he vanished into the trees.

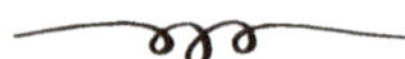

Conservation work and community development will play an increasingly important role in the future. Like two sides of the same coin, they mutually reinforce and influence one another. Conservation work must benefit the communities who live near or within the scope of conservation efforts, so that both can work together in harmony and support meaningful, long-term action.

Community development is not about charity. It's far better not to give handouts at all than to take away someone's rights. Instead, we should focus on helping people reclaim what is rightfully theirs. The goal is not to give from a position of privilege, but to restore the rights of the less fortunate, so they can stand on equal footing.

Jacky has taught me that all people—indeed, all of God's creations—are equal, each granted the same inherent rights. Our support should not stem from a sense of superiority or power, but from the recognition that these individuals are just like us: human beings, granted with the same rights and dignity.

So, my father's message still holds true, even though the way I phrase it has changed, 'Don't speak of conservation or the integrity of creation while people are still hungry. Act from a place of love, not pity. Only then can we regard all humans as equally worthy, each possessing dignity, power, and equal rights.'

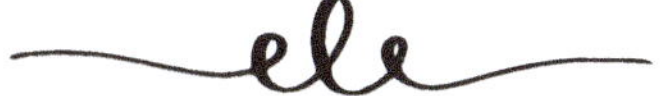

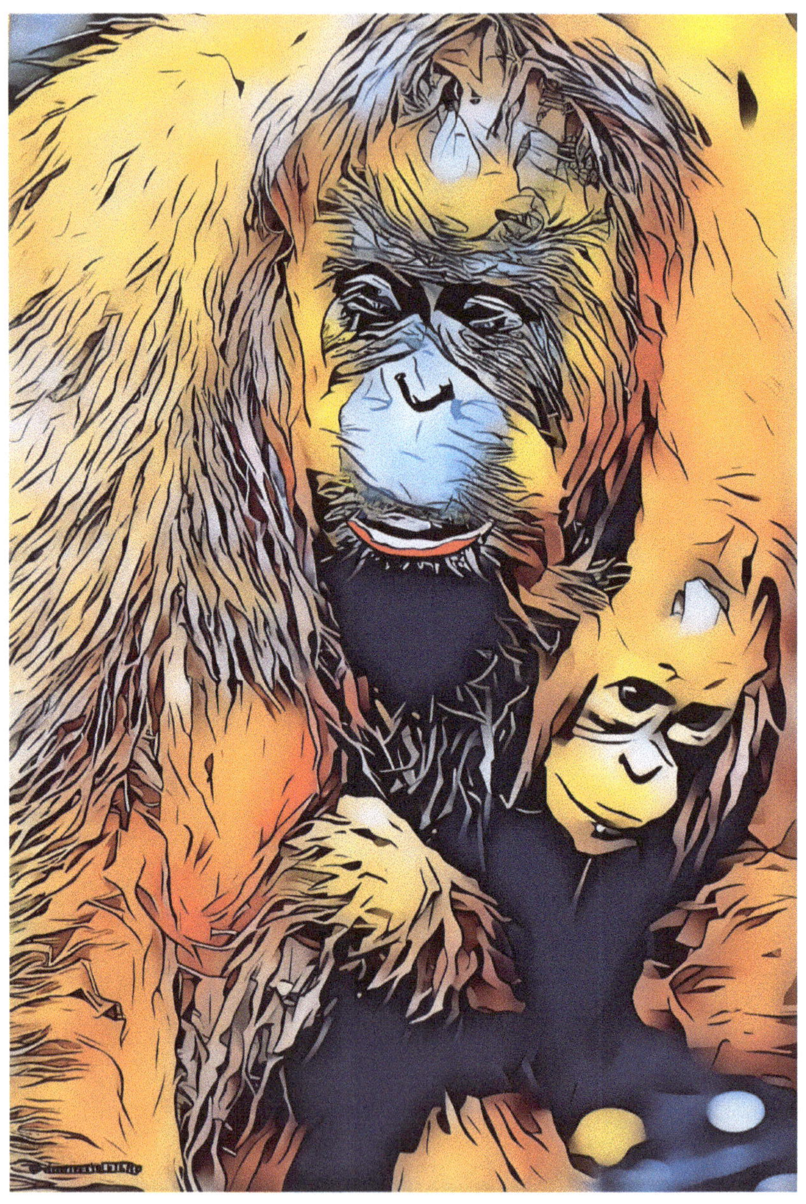

"One close friend
who understands the meaning of your tears
is more valuable than
thousands of colleagues who only know your smile."

Chapter 12

Impaired yet Unbounded Together

One day, as the sun beat down with its fiery intensity, I saw a blind man at an intersection being gently guided by a boy who seemed to be his son. Both were barefoot. I couldn't imagine the pain they must have felt on the soles of their feet, walking on the scorching hot road. Their lives seemed so difficult, and survival a constant struggle. But as I passed by, I was surprised to see there were no signs of hardship on their faces. Both father and son appeared to be at peace with their simple lives. Jokes were being exchanged, laughter peppering their conversation.

As I continued my journey, my thoughts turned to the many disabled orangutans at the Borneo Orangutan Survival Foundation (BOSF) rehabilitation centers, particularly Kopral and Shelton at Samboja Lestari in East Kalimantan, Indonesia. Their unique friendship serves as a powerful example for our team.

Many people believe that the BOSF team draws inspiration from certain exceptional individuals. Unfortunately, they couldn't be more wrong. Our true inspiration—a sentiment shared across the broader Orangutan Foundation network—comes from the unwavering bond and determination between Kopral and Shelton to support each other.

Despite their disabilities, Kopral, who lost both arms, and Shelton, who is blind, worked together with remarkable determination to learn new skills, demonstrating that the greatest challenges can be overcome with teamwork. If they can do it, why can't those of us without physical limitations work together as well as they do?

While I was still thinking about the two special orangutans, a vision of Kopral flashed through my mind. He started a conversation with me.

"Hey, what's up with you? Thinking about us at the Forest School, huh?" Kopral asked, his voice tinged with amusement.

"Yes, I am. And I envy your close friendship with Shelton. Your bond of solidarity with him isn't based on your strengths, but rather on your weaknesses and impairments. Meanwhile, we humans tend to think about helping others only when we have an abundance of resources. Worse yet, our good deeds are often misunderstood," I said.

"Never regret being kind to the wrong people. Your actions speak volumes about your character, just as theirs do about them. As the Greek philosopher Socrates once said: "Doing injustice is more shameful than suffering injustice." This is the belief I hold on to, even when I suffer injustice at the hands of humans—whether it was when I was taken away from my mother and made into their pet, or when we were physically harmed by human actions," he explained.

Their story is deeply moving. Kopral was not just talking in theory; he was truly using his own life as an example.

When they were younger, despite losing both of his arms to electrocution, Kopral eagerly helped Shelton, who was blinded by air rifle pellets, out of his enclosure so they could join in play and learn survival skills at the Forest School at the Rehabilitation Center.

Sadly, after Kopral graduated from Forest School, the blind Shelton had to return to the enclosure for his own safety. Meanwhile, Kopral, now living on a sanctuary island within the rehabilitation center, continues to navigate the forest and negotiate difficult terrain, thanks to the skills he learned at Forest School. As a result, the two friends can no longer play together.

Yet, their bond remains unbroken. Even though they now live apart, Kopral continues to regularly visit his friend, Shelton, at his enclosure. Their friendship, forged over the many years at Forest School, has not been lessened by the separation. Kopral usually visits Shelton around lunchtime, sometimes bringing his own lunch to Shelton's compound so they can eat together! It's heartwarming to witness the closeness between these two very special orangutans.

Although Kopral and Shelton have required additional love and care due to the disabilities that prevent them from living freely in the forest, their story of friendship serves as a wonderful example of the spirit of kindness, collaborative effort, and mutual support in overcoming adversity. This is why they are an inspiration to us all.

"So why are you as calm as the Pacific Ocean, my friend?" asked Kopral.

I was too embarrassed to admit that I envied the strong sense of camaraderie he shared with Shelton. But this time I had to acknowledge that they were better than us humans at showing loyalty and being supportive of each other.

"I am just thinking. Why can't we be like you and Shelton?" I replied. "Even though you have no arms and Shelton is blind, both of you manage to support each other in overcoming your challenges. In contrast, those of us without physical impairments are often reluctant to help one another. Even when you suffer injustice, you don't respond in kind."

"You see, here's the thing," he said sagely, adopting the posture of a philosopher as he began his lecture, "While many people think about changing the world, few consider changing themselves first. Let your good deeds be a way to express gratitude to your Creator. Don't waste time blaming yourself or others for injustices or circumstances you never could have imagined. Instead, be introspective and reflect on your life to gain insights on how to improve. The purpose of life is to remind one another to be kind, not to point fingers and blame each other's shortcomings. If we solely live for the approval of others, we will perish from their rejection. After all, conservation work is a service to God and the natural world."

"Wow, why do you sound like a sufi, Kopral?" I said. "Where did you learn to give advice?"

"Humans!" he exclaimed. "Always assuming that when we offer suggestions, it's because we are lecturing, telling you what to do, or preaching—when all we want to do is help. In truth, we orangutans pay closer attention to nature and its wisdom, which enables us to absorb and understand your conversations," he said calmly.

"That's certainly true," I agreed. "However, we often feel as though the work we do in conservation is full of blood, sweat, and tears, and fraught with disappointment. Many of our partners and colleagues withdraw their support and even abandon us when adversity strikes."

"What's with the resentment and complaints, my friend?" he asked.

He was right. I admit I was disheartened and exhausted at the time, which was why the complaints slipped out.

"Realize that having just one close friend who understands the meaning of your tears is far more valuable than having thousands of colleagues who only know your smile," he said wisely.

"Is this what you meant when you told me about your friendship with Shelton?" I asked.

"My friendship with Shelton is nothing special," he replied, then continued. "Knowing our own limitations is important so that we don't become overconfident in life. That's the lesson we learned from our physical limitations. Not everyone who owns a guitar automatically becomes a guitarist, right? Many people have hands and eyes, but they don't use them well. The Scriptures say, "If your hand causes you to sin, cut it off. It is better to enter heaven with one hand than to go to hell with your body intact," he continued empathetically, his voice rising.

"Yes, your life with Shelton and how you both support each other despite your limitations really inspires our work," I said.

"No one can change the past, but everyone can change their future, my friend," said Kopral with a smile. His smile struck me deeply, a silent reminder of how often we lacked the resolve to face challenges--shying away from problems, even though doing so never brought us closer to solutions. "Make peace with the limitations you have, my friend, and remember that running away from a problem will not solve it," he said as he walked away slowly.

As he disappeared into the surroundings, I heard his soft, almost inaudible voice: "Try to understand what is, not how it should be. Understanding the world as it is, rather than how you believe it should be, will teach you to become wiser."

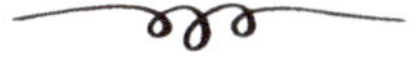

Listening to Kopral was like listening to my father; our conversations were casual but filled with life's insights. He pointed out that most of us aren't grateful for what we have and are constantly dissatisfied with what we haven't accomplished.

Kopral and Shelton showed us that our limitations don't have to prevent us from striving and doing good, because true victory does not come from never losing, but from being able to get back up after falling. Just like my father's wise advice, which still rings true for me: "In living this life, don't stop when you're tired; stop when you're done."

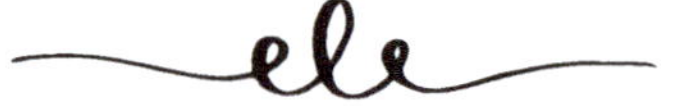

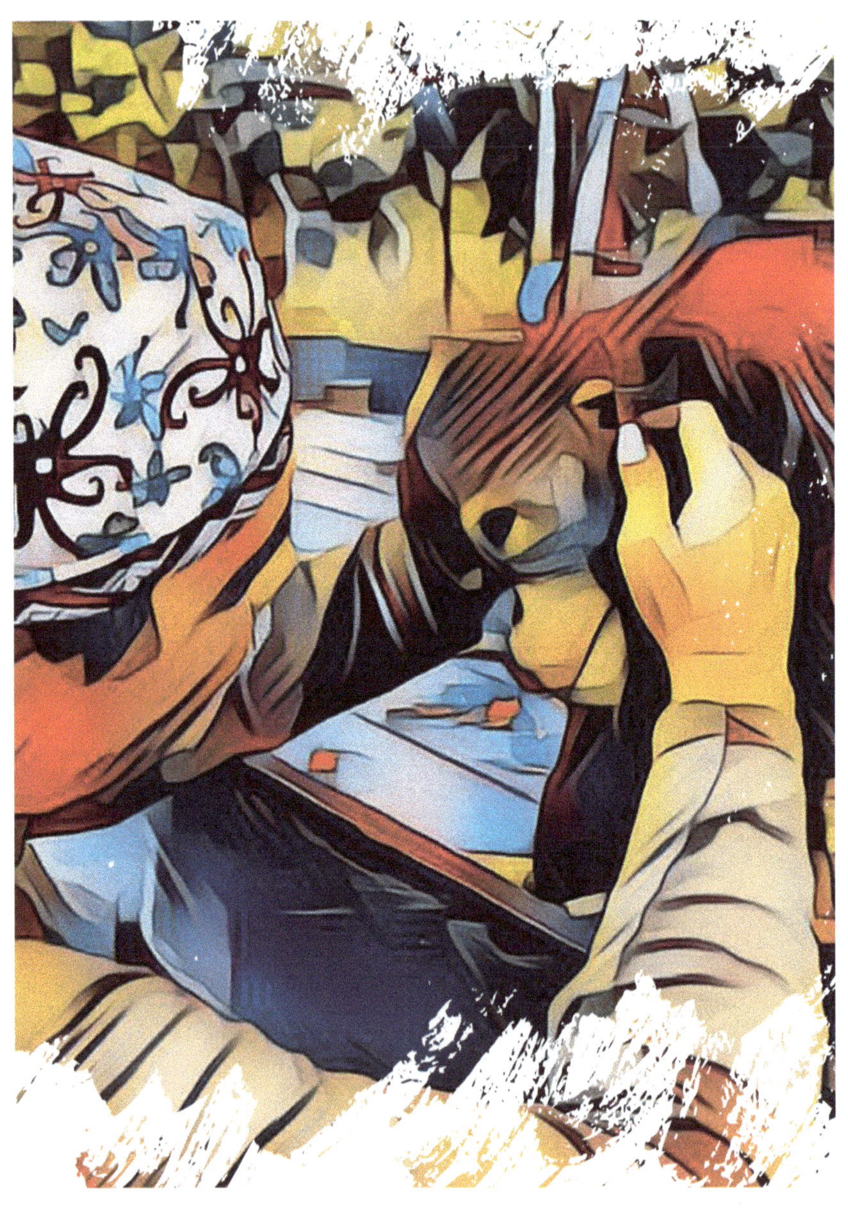

*"Let go of worries about tomorrow,
for it will bring its own challenges.
Let today's challenges be enough for today"*

Chapter 13

Everything will be Okay

During the rainy season, unwinding with a cup of hot, unsweetened black coffee in the afternoon, while listening to the gentle pitter-patter of rain, is often considered a luxury. But on that particular day, my mind was consumed with thoughts of the disappearing forest and the hundreds of orangutans still confined in cages, unable to return home to the forest.

While nature allowed us to relax, entertaining us with the soothing rhythm of the rain, the music player on my laptop drifted until it landed on 'Everything's Okay' sung by the female artist Lenka. The lyrics of the song took me down memory lane, reminding me of our orangutan release process:

> *Keep giving me hope for a better day,*
> *Keep giving me love to find a way,*
> *Through this heaviness I feel,*
> *I just need someone to say,*
> *Everything's okay...*

That song reminded me of Tarzan, the first orangutan we released into the wild after a decade-long hiatus. I recalled how heavily it had rained the night before he was flown to Bukit Batikap Protection Forest in Central Kalimantan by helicopter. Throughout the night, I offered a prayer, hoping the rain would stop by morning so that he could be released. Flipping through my memories of Tarzan brought him vividly to mind, and soon, an imaginary conversation unfolded between us, where we exchanged stories about the songs of the rain and the latest news from the forest.

"Hey! Long time no see! How's your coffee and the song, my friend?" Tarzan greeted me warmly. He truly was a friend, one of the orangutans in our care whom we hadn't seen in a long time.

"Lenka's song, accompanied by the sound of the afternoon rain, reminded me of your release process during that rainy season."

"Yes, I remember," he replied. "Thanks to the help of the helicopter, you were able to do frequent releases. Each time, more than ten orangutans were returned to the forest," he added. He seemed to be quite aware of what we were doing and who was present at Bukit Batikap Protection Forest at that time.

"That's right, Tarzan. Back then, we were able to release large numbers of orangutans frequently. But now, we're struggling to find helicopters and secure funding," I said, sharing my woes with him.

"You know, God always has a good reason for derailing our plans and not giving us what we want. So, we shouldn't pray only when we're in need or facing difficulty, but also when we experience great joy or prosperity," he commented, trying to soothe my discontent.

What he had just told me stopped me in my tracks. I thought to myself: '*Have we forgotten to express our gratitude when the release process went smoothly? Or, perhaps, have we been complaining too much?*'

He continued, "Understand that orangutan conservation will always be like a rollercoaster ride, my friend. It requires extra effort to save my kind, especially with the limitations we face. But you should also know that no matter how great the challenges you and your colleagues encounter in orangutan and habitat conservation, you can choose to wake up each day with joy and gratitude to God for His grace. Never forget that some people have it worse than you. Some are still struggling to survive. Perhaps those of you working in orangutan conservation should remember the advice of Ovidio, a Roman poet, who said, '*Saepe creat molles aspera spina rosas*'—'often the prickly thorn produces tender roses.'"

"Thank you for your advice, Tarzan. It is worth exploring what we can accomplish despite the current limitations," I replied firmly.

"We often desire what we don't have. Think about it, most of us are dissatisfied with what we have. I'm one of those who often feel envious when I see others experiencing good fortune or owning things of value. Immediately, I feel like I should have the same. However, this tendency is toxic, and holding onto this mindset in life won't bring us true happiness." Once again, he offered insightful advice.

"But the uncertainty of future releases—due to the lack of helicopters and insufficient funds—makes me undeniably angry because it pains me to see the long queue of orangutans who can't be released yet," I grumbled, voicing my frustration once again.

"'*Iracundiam qui vincit, hostem superat maximum*'— 'He who conquers his anger triumphs over his greatest enemy,' said Publilius Syrus in 251 CE. So, it's okay to feel anger, as long as it doesn't lead to missed opportunities," he commented sagely. "However, facing challenges—no matter the issue—is how we develop and learn. Yes, adversity can be stifling, and understandably, we want it to end quickly. But going through the process will make us better people. So, you must be resilient and persevere, my friend."

"Now, let's consider the options available given the constraints. When there's no helicopter, but there's a long line of orangutans still waiting to be released, you will undoubtedly try to find alternative ways to release them— such as using cars and boats, right?" he suggested.

"Yes, but this approach has its pros and cons due to the high risks involved," I replied.

"Have you ever heard of John Lennon?" he asked unexpectedly, once again surprising me with his knowledge.

I felt a surge of annoyance. I thought: *'Who doesn't know John Lennon and his band, The Beatles?'* I replied, "I like The Beatles, but what does that have to do with our current dilemma? Using cars and boats for the release would extend the schedule from one day to two or three days. And that comes with a significant risk."

"Ah, my friend, this just proves you have more to learn," he joked, laughing heartily. "So, as John Lennon once said, 'Everything will be okay in the end. If it's not okay, then it's not the end.' This implies that if things aren't going well, you must continue to fight. Often, we waste so much energy by exaggerating small issues. Remember what the Roman philosopher Seneca once said: *'Vivere militare est,'* which means 'to live is to fight.' The Bible also says that God will not give you challenges beyond what you can bear. So, in essence, life is a struggle. We clearly can't calm the storm, so stop trying. All we can do is to calm ourselves, and that way, the storm will pass. Or would you prefer a more sarcastic take on adversity from Winston Churchill? Here's what he said: 'Always remember, when you're going through hell, keep going.' Hahaha..." he said, laughing out loud.

"Thank you Tarzan," I replied, feeling chastised. "There isn't a day that goes by without something beyond our control happening. It could be bad weather, a person with a short temper, or a partner who's unwilling to collaborate. As you said, the only thing we can control is our attitude toward challenges. It's this mindset that shapes the future because, ultimately, there is no such thing as a risk-free life. Isn't that right, my friend?"

"Exactly. As Marcus Aurelius, one of the greatest Roman emperors, said, 'Is your cucumber bitter? Throw it away. Are there briars in your path? Turn aside. That's enough for you to know. Do not go on and say, "Why are these unpleasant things brought into the world?"' Those who understand life will laugh at you for always asking why. Just accept the situation and deal with the issue in front of you. So, back to our topic—what are you going to do with the release program?" Tarzan asked with interest.

"So, instead of the usual one-day process by helicopter, a release using cars and boats will take two to three days. To test this, we'll conduct a trial run with one orangutan and a small, specialized team. Every step of the journey—from the starting point to the destination—will be meticulously documented: where we stop, why we stop, the condition of the orangutan at each point, and the condition of all the boats used. Everything will be double-checked and recorded. The team must also bring a knockdown cage for transit—similar in size to those at the rehabilitation center but easy to dismantle—in case of unforeseen weather changes that could cause delays. In such a situation, the orangutan will be temporarily moved from the transport cage to the transit cage to ensure its health and well-being. We must also consider and test the possibility of the transport cage being thrown into the river during the journey. So, not only must the humans wear life jackets, but the transport cage will also need some type of 'life jacket' or flotation device to ensure its safety.

"Well, then, how do you test the one for the cage?" he asked eagerly.

"Ah... be a little patient, my friend," I replied to a hasty Tarzan, who couldn't wait to hear about it. This was a natural question for him to ask, because, when the time came, his friends would also be placed in the transport cage. His concern stemmed from a genuine desire to ensure his friends' safety.

"First, we'll have this special life jacket made from a large piece of styrofoam shaped like a half-cylinder, which will be attached to both the left and right sides of the transport cage. Then, the cage will be filled with rocks weighing 1.5 times the body weight of the heaviest orangutan available. After that, we'll submerge the cage in a deep, fast-flowing river to test whether it stays afloat. As long as more than half of the cage remains above the water's surface, we can safely assume it will. For the next test, we'll consult the manufacturer of the life jacket for safety assurances about their product. Once we have this assurance, we'll have some volunteers from our team sit inside the cage while it's submerged in the river."

"Wow, that's pretty extreme," he laughed, covering his face with his palms and shaking his head in disbelief.

"It is never our intention to be cruel, Tarzan. But, if we're not confident in what we're doing, then our lives are at stake. Do you realize that all of us who work at BOSF (Borneo Orangutan Survival Foundation) value each orangutan's life as much as our own? That's why we test for every potential risk. Only after all of the tests are completed will we conduct a trial release. If that's successful, we can start releasing orangutans in batches. After all, isn't life a cyclical ebb and flow? If the good times pass, so will the bad, right?"

"Ah, you're finally getting wiser," Tarzan said, laughing heartily.

"Well, we only have one life to live. Therefore, we should live it to the fullest. No matter how simple the task, let's give it our all, so that our efforts today become the beautiful memories of tomorrow that we'll remember with a smile."

"Absolutely. Even the darkest night ends, and the sun rises again," Tarzan said, swinging away, disappearing into the dense forest.

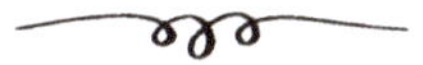

As the afternoon wore on unnoticed, the tune playing on my music player shifted to "Ya Sudahlah" (It's Alright) by Bondan and Fade2Black:

Apapun yang terjadi,
(Whatever happens)

Ku 'kan selalu ada untukmu,
(I'll always be there for you)

Janganlah kau bersedih,
(Don't you be sad)

'Cause everything's gonna be okay...

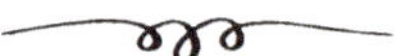

Tarzan taught us there's a silver lining to every challenge—the good that comes from adversity. The future isn't determined by the lines on our palms; even those without hands still have a future. Success isn't something others can decide for us, but something we must strive toward and create. So, we must give our best in everything we do to achieve success. We don't need to wait for the perfect moment to start; now is the best time to take the first steps toward our future. Once we start, the doors to our dreams will open.

Therefore, let us be grateful in all circumstances. While the storm may rage now, the rain doesn't last forever. So, let go of worries about tomorrow, for it will bring its own challenges. Let today's challenges be enough for today.

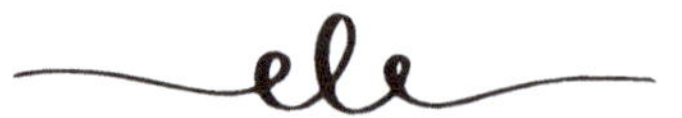

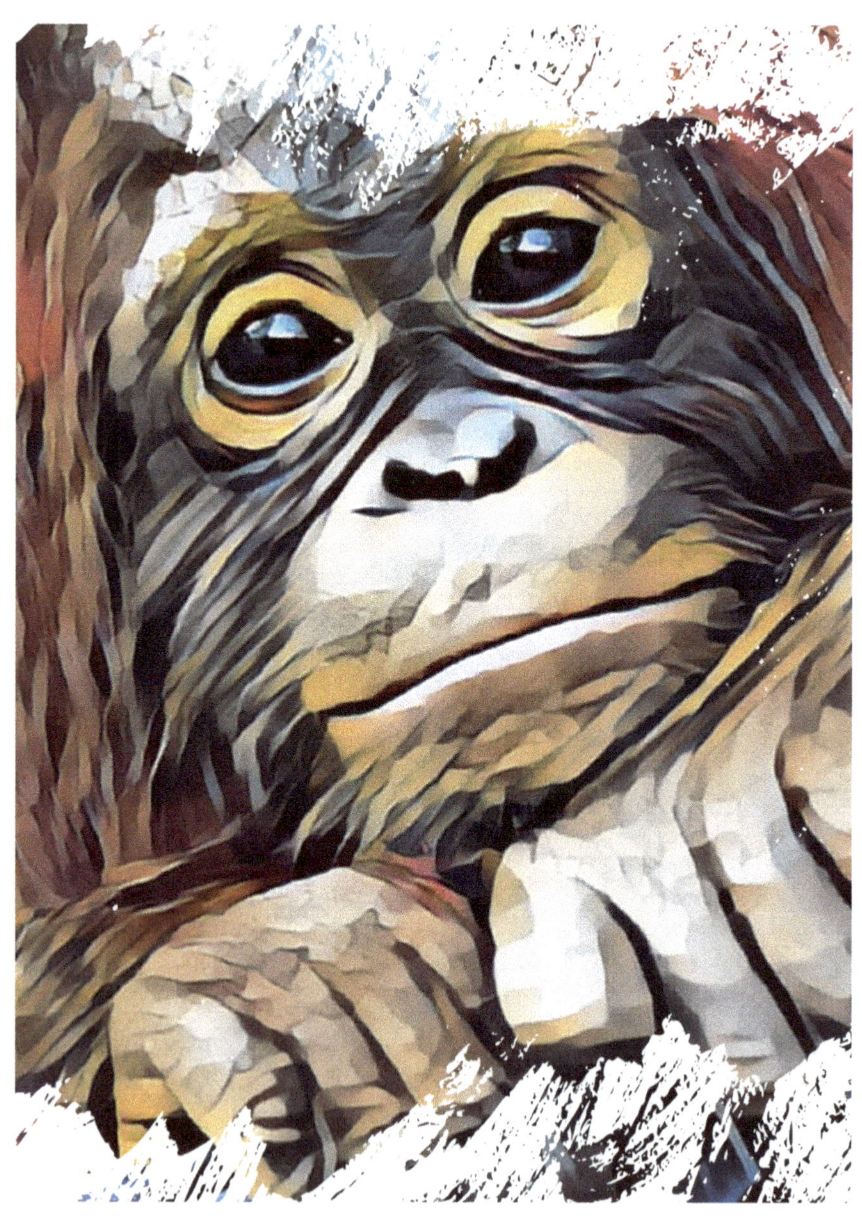

"Falling in love is common.
Staying in love, however,
is what's truly extraordinary."

Chapter 14

Love Liberates

That afternoon at the monitoring camp, the rain fell heavier than usual, as if God were pouring as much water as possible from the sky. As I sat in the corner of the monitoring hut, sipping a cup of bitter coffee, I savored the rhythm of the raindrops, the sound of the rushing river, and the swishing wind that made the trees in the forest dance together.

Due to the rain, we were forced to take shelter at the camp and postpone the orangutan release operation, as continuing to navigate the slippery, steep road would be too dangerous—both for the team carrying the cage and for the orangutan itself. This is a situation we often face during the release process. Although our team frequently works in hazardous conditions, the expression *'vivere pericoloso'*—'to live dangerously,' as it is commonly known—reminds us that every risk we encounter in the field must still be carefully considered.

While watching the leaves dance to the rhythm of the wind, I spotted an orangutan we had released several years prior—named Juki—sitting in one of the trees, enjoying the rain. His face looked so radiant and animated, as if every raindrop recharged his energy and enlivened him.

After witnessing this unique phenomenon, I couldn't wait to greet him. "Hello, Juki! Why are you playing in the rain? Take shelter, or you might catch a cold," I said, expressing my concern. I felt I had the right to worry, considering we had cared for him and looked after him at the BOSF (Borneo Orangutan Survival Foundation) Nyaru Menteng Rehabilitation Center in Central Kalimantan for many years, and had painstakingly brought him back to the forest.

Juki ignored my concerns and kept playing instead. At some point, he stopped and asked, "What exactly are you worried about? Weren't we created to be in the forest and become one with nature?"

I paused and reflected. *Wow*, what was wrong with me that I was so worried about an orangutan who had already returned to his home?

His response brought back memories from many years ago when I traveled to seek support for orangutan conservation in various countries. On those trips, from one city to another, I often shared stories of the accomplishments we've made with the support of our overseas partners. I also showed videos and discussed the challenges and difficulties of caring for orangutans. Of course, the blood, sweat, and tears we invested in our orangutan conservation journey were woven into these tales, as were the joy and sorrow that intertwined with every breath and step we took—from rescuing orangutans in conflict zones to their eventual release back into nature.

"Hey, why have you gone so quiet? Where has your mind wandered off to that you're not present in your body?" chided Juki.

I jolted from my reverie—lost in the trip down memory lane, recalling how I moved from one city to another, conducting outreach—or as I jokingly refer to it in Indonesian, *'ngamen'* (busking)—through various countries to raise funds and gain support for orangutan protection. I also found myself lost in a sea of memories, including being asked questions by colleagues and partners that were beyond my expectations.

"Hmm, nowhere really. I was just remembering my overseas travels to different countries and how often I had to answer questions I never imagined before," I said, smiling at him.

He gave me a penetrating look from across the distance. Tilting his head slightly, as if puzzled, he said, "Isn't life always full of surprises? Shouldn't your frequent trips to and from the forest, and your immersion in the energy of nature God has provided, make you calmer in answering even the most difficult questions? After all, as Socrates once said, 'Only to those with refined feelings does God reveal the beauty and secrets of nature.' But, if I may ask, what questions did they ask, and what was your answer?" he asked curiously.

Yes, that's how my orangutan friends have always been—never passing up an opportunity to gain new information while simultaneously offering me their own insights.

I told him that I was reminded of the time when we were raising awareness about orangutans, especially during our travels abroad. On each visit, we usually shared the latest stories from the forest, including our conservation achievements and the goals we were pursuing. We also invited the audience to watch a short video showcasing our work in preparing orangutan candidates for their return to the forest, from preparation to release. This video documented each stage in the release process, beginning with our team's efforts to prepare an orangutan candidate for release—such as the final health check before the orangutan was transported from the rehabilitation center to the forest. It also covered the re-checking of the orangutan's health every two hours during the journey, all the way to the final moment when the orangutan's cage door was opened upon arrival at the designated forest location.

After watching the video on the orangutan release, audience members eagerly asked me questions. "Why didn't you cry when you released the orangutans? Even though the BOSF team had cared for them for years, why didn't you seem to be sad when they were finally released into the wild?" asked one person, curious to know.

I was so startled by the question that I fell silent. Should we have cried when our orangutan friends were released, or should we have laughed? The question unsettled me.

I was so taken aback that I needed a moment to think before responding. If I had answered with 'crying', the next question might have been, "Why did you cry when the orangutans were now free?" On the other hand, If we had laughed in happiness to see the orangutans free, the next question might have been, "Why weren't you sad?" or "Why did it seem like there's no emotional bond?"

Honestly, I was at a loss for how to answer at the time. My mind was flooded with questions. Then, I closed my eyes, regulated my breath, and prayed. My prayer was simple: "God, guide me to respond well."

Once I finished praying, I felt calmer and was able to answer. I said, "As a father, I will answer these questions from a father's perspective. So, what would happen if, at God's appointed time, we had to walk our daughter down the aisle for her wedding? Would you laugh or cry? I'm sure almost all of you would cry tears of joy. It's possible that those in attendance might even record the moment when our tears well up. But, even if it isn't visible, the 'pool of tears' might be stored in the heart. And if you ask me again, 'Why do you have to cry?' I'd respond, 'Because my daughter has grown up, and on that very day, she will begin her life with the person who loves her.'"

I paused before continuing, "Then, if I ask myself, am I 100% sure that her partner will love her 100%, as much as I do, as her father? I would answer: I'm not 100% sure. However, because my daughter has reached the stage of life where she is entering into a matrimonial union and starting her own family, it is my duty and responsibility before God to walk her down the aisle. Therefore, as a father, I will send her off with tears of joy."

"Afterward, will I cry in front of others or in front of my daughter?" I said contemplatively. "Probably not, but that doesn't mean I'm not shedding happy tears. Similarly, this example illustrates the complex mix of emotions I felt when we released an orangutan—who had spent years confined in a cage—back into the wild after a lengthy process of care and rehabilitation."

"Our tears of joy may not always be seen or captured on camera, but that's the feeling we experience every time we see an orangutan free," I explained to him. Without my noticing, a single warm tear rolled down my cheek as I spoke. I hastily wiped it away.

"Love liberates, my friend," Juki assured me. "If you love someone, give them freedom; that is the true essence of love. Love is not just gentleness, generosity, or pure goodness, whether given with or without conditions. Love is also the act of sharing, understanding, giving, liberating, offering, and responding to a Higher Calling. In essence, love is life exalted. The Chinese philosopher Lao Tzu once wrote, 'To be loved deeply by someone gives you strength, while to love someone deeply gives you courage.' And we orangutans see that in you; we feel and recognize the love in what you do—to return us to freedom and independence in our home in the forest."

"Thank you, Juki," I said.

"Any other interesting questions to learn from?" he asked with a smile on his face.

"Of course there are, but let's just focus on this one, Juki," I replied.

"By the way, why are you still working in orangutan conservation? Why are you still fighting to secure forests that will serve as homes for orangutans? Isn't all that difficult?" he asked.

This is the most frequently asked question, so I gave him the same response I've always given: "Our deepest desire to bring about freedom for the orangutans drives us to feel that we are moving in the right direction. It doesn't matter if others disagree, because this is a calling from the core of our hearts and minds to help orangutans— it's something we simply can't ignore. For us, making incremental progress is better than perfection. It's not uncommon for people to accuse us of not caring about the quality of our work because we're too focused on achieving our goals," I explained to Juki, the orangutan, who was still happily playing in the rain while listening to my chatter.

"Putting others down will not make you better than them, you know," he commented.

What Juki said was true, but unfortunately, we humans often fail to pay much attention to this. This contrasts sharply with BOSF's work philosophy, where we strive to be better every day, always evolving without criticizing or discrediting others.

He continued his musings: "The best person is not the one with the perfect brain, but the one who can make the best use of the less-perfect parts of his brain." His words reflected an Aristotelian concept, reminding me that despite our human flaws, we can still accomplish great things.

"Why so contemplative, my friend?" he chided, noticing I had drifted off. Indeed, I was lost in my memories of studying the Philosophy of Science in college.

"Sorry, I feel like I'm listening to a lecture from you. And the audience's question is always the same: 'Why are you still so keen on working in orangutan conservation?'" I replied, referring to his earlier question.

"Perhaps the person asking should learn about what Khalil Gibran said about love," he suggested.

"What do you mean?" I asked, impressed by his wealth of knowledge. I wondered when and how the wind and the rustling leaves of this forest had taught him these things.

"'It's easier to fall in love than to maintain love,' so says Khalil Gibran. Or perhaps you should read the works of Marcus Fabius Quintilianus, also known simply as Quintilian, a famous Roman rhetorician from Hispania, whose works deeply influenced the rhetorical schools in the Middle Ages and Renaissance literature. He wrote a sentence that might serve as a fitting depiction of the choices you and your colleagues at BOSF, who remain determined to work in conservation despite other temptations: '*Facilius est fine facere quam diu*,' meaning 'It is easier to do many things than to do one for a long time,'" he said.

"Thank you, Juki. We'll continue to put in the effort. But we have a finite lifespan, and nothing lasts forever," I said, launching into a new argument. I had to make sure that any orangutans who might expect us to live forever, advocate for them, and continue to work for them for eternity, would understand otherwise. But, through our consistent efforts, we are at the very least trying to emulate the steadfastness of a rock, as Aurelius, one of Rome's benevolent emperors, once said: "Be like the rock that the waves keep crashing over. It stands unmoved, and the raging of the sea falls still around it."

For once, Juki seemed to ignore my words. He began moving, swinging from tree to tree, away from where I was sitting in the corner of the monitoring hut, quietly saying, "I choose to live a short life, one full of meaning and work, rather than a long life that is empty." After that, he darted even faster toward higher branches, disappearing behind a thicket of trees that were still drenched in rain.

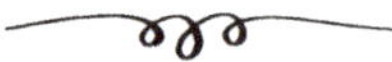

Love liberates and must be fought for. And that's the reason God created humans—to be messengers of love to all of creation. It is love that motivates everyone at BOSF to keep working and remain committed to the cause, even though life in orangutan conservation is like a roller-coaster ride—

jarring, with ups, downs, turns, and sudden drops from great heights. Truly, there have been countless unexpected surprises. But none of it really matters, because, as Mohandas K. Gandhi once said: "As long as there is love, there is life."

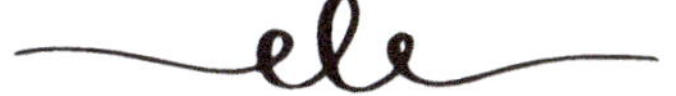

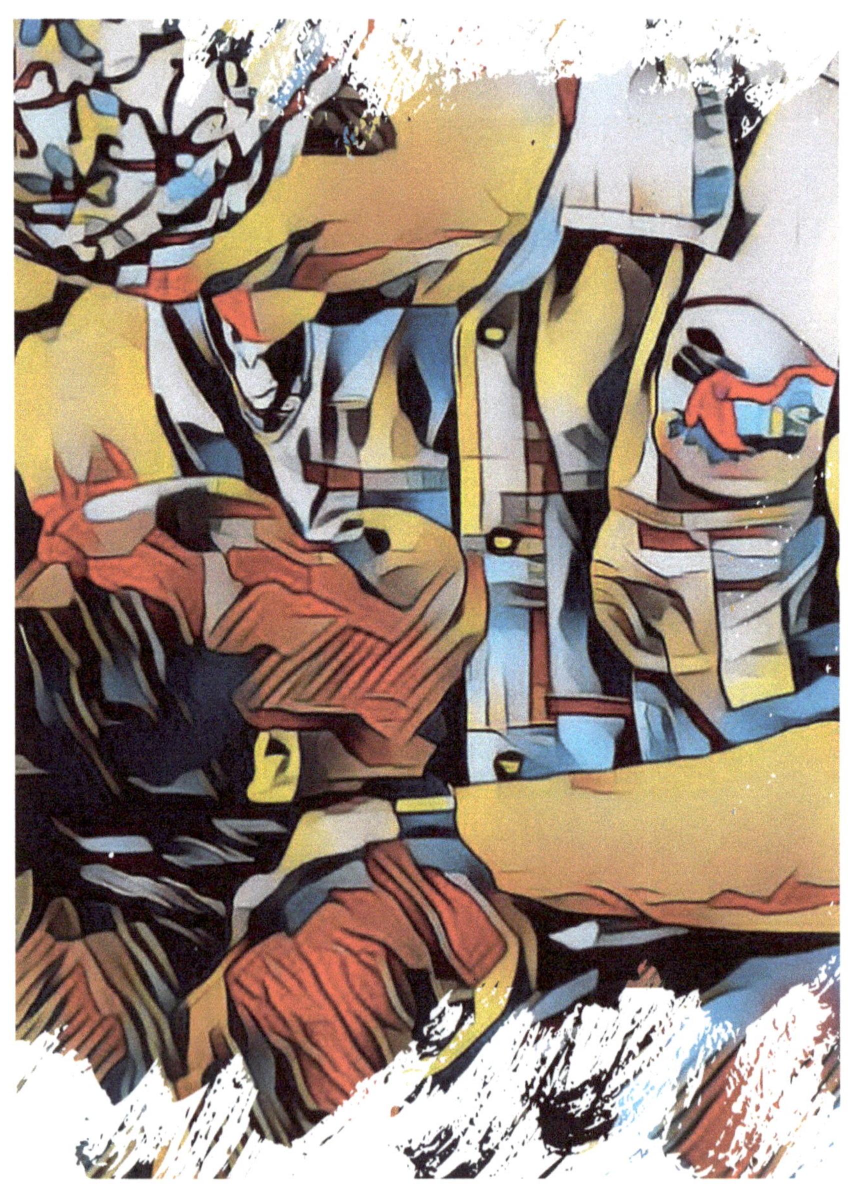

*How could we
not long for the towering tree crown?*

*How could we
forget the hornbill's love song?*

*How could we
weave our nests from behind these bars?*

*How could you claim to care
for the fate of orangutans,*

If you don't protect the forest of their homes?

-RWW-

Chapter 15

Never Lose Hope

In Kamus Besar Bahasa Indonesia, the official dictionary of the Indonesian language, the definition of the word "harap" (hope) is: to request, to wish, or a desire for something to happen, usually for something that fulfills a need or a longing. So, what can we understand about hope? The definition implies that, first, hope is a strong anchor, and second, it provides peace, comfort, and safety to the soul.

We must be able to differentiate between hope and desire. "Desire" emphasizes actions and attitudes driven by the human ego. It means that any outcome must align with our thoughts, desires, and expectations. "Hope," on the other hand, refers to the attitude, response, and actions of waiting for assistance and compassion from others who possess greater competence, power, and ability to help us. This reflects a mindset of depending on others beyond ourselves. In other words, we are entirely reliant on others to help us realize our hope and bring it to fruition.

While sitting in a corner of a dimly lit room at the orangutan monitoring camp in the heart of Borneo's wilderness, my thoughts drifted to the rows of cages housing unreleasable orangutans at the BOSF (Borneo Orangutan Survival Foundation) rehabilitation center. I recalled the faces of the orangutans on the pre-release islands, their expressions filled with doubt. I also remembered the day I saw an orangutan hanging from a large tree branch while accompanying the monitoring team at the pre-release island of BOSF's Samboja Lestari Rehabilitation Center in East Kalimantan. That orangutan gave me a long look as we watched each other closely. I recognized her—her name was Lesley. Her gaze pierced my heart, sharper than the sharpest sword in the world.

Then I heard someone speak to me. "Hey, you. Yes, you. Why does your body language suggest that you're reluctant to monitor us on this pre-release island?"

I was startled and searched for the source of the voice. I asked a colleague on monitoring duty if he had heard anything, but he said he hadn't.

"Hey, human. Yes, you. Use your senses and your heart to listen to our voice—the voice of nature that you humans should pay attention to. Yes, it's me, an orangutan, speaking to you right now."

I was surprised. To listen more closely, I regulated my breath, slowing down my inhalations and exhalations to calm myself. I focused on absorbing the serenity of nature and allowed the rhythm of my heartbeat to synchronize with the symphony of rippling water and the rustling wind playing with the leaves. Time seemed to pass very slowly. Every pore in my body felt filled with oxygen, and the bright light emanating from me, the surrounding nature, and the orangutan intertwined, forming one luminous sphere that radiated in all directions.

Then, "Oh, hello, Lesley! Forgive me," I said. "I was too preoccupied with my own thoughts." As we continued gazing into each other's eyes, we began a conversation. Unbeknownst to me at the time, that roller coaster of a discussion would take me on a ride of emotional highs and lows.

"So, what's weighing on your mind? What has been troubling you since you arrived at this Rehabilitation Center and started observing us here on this pre-release island?" she asked sympathetically.

"This Rehabilitation Center shouldn't be responsible for housing so many caged and pre-release orangutans. Hundreds have graduated from Forest School, yet they are returned to their cages so the younger ones can learn in the forest. If this trend continues, where is this conservation effort heading, and what does it really accomplish? Where will it end? These are the thoughts that have been consuming my mind, my friend."

"Aha, I finally get to hear your frustration. Remember, there are several things that give humans the resilience to face adversity: faith, hope, and love."

"As for matters concerning us orangutans, come on… there's still hope. There is still much you can do." She smiled, as though hoping her words would ease my mind and strengthen my resolve.

I fell silent for a moment. My thoughts drifted back to a time in my childhood when I was frustrated, and my father tried to reassure me with words of hope. And now, I found myself having to learn the same from an orangutan.

"But this pattern has been going on for years," I complained to her. "Rescuing orangutans and bringing them to the rehabilitation center is very easy, but don't even ask how difficult it is to release them back into the forest. And whenever I visit the enclosures, I can't bear to see the male orangutans' empty, spiritless eyes, as though they have given up all hope. You understand what I mean. Those orangutans will never comprehend why they have to live in cages, just as they will never understand how humans can be so callous as to murder their mothers, then smuggle and transport them out of the country to be sold."

"Yes, indeed, you humans are the ones who have uprooted us from our *fitrah*—our natural state. And even though it is also true that many of us are frustrated and appear to have lost hope, this is precisely the point at which we need you to play your part in helping us leave our cages and live among the trees."

"Well, therein lies the problem. It is not as simple as you say, especially since the number of orangutans at the Center continues to increase," I told her.

"So, I hear humans are intelligent creatures, but why don't I see that intelligence matched with the wisdom of the heart?" she scoffed. "Well, listen. Let me tell you something. You've driven a car, right? Have you ever wondered why the car's rearview mirror is always smaller than the windshield? Now, imagine the rearview mirror as the past and the windshield as the future. Which direction do you want to go? Do you want to move forward or go backward? So come on, just use the rearview mirror occasionally—to exercise prudence when you are looking back at the past, but remain focused on moving forward into the future. The past has already left its mark on history—use it to avoid making future mistakes. Don't dwell in the sentimentality and nostalgia of the past, let alone lamenting past failures while seeking justification. While it is important to examine the past, the goal lies ahead."

"Wait, wait, where is this conversation going?" I asked, bewildered. "Why are you making pointed comments like that? Are you blaming my kind for the adversity you're facing because you've been uprooted from *fitrah* (natural state)?"

"All right, let's not judge people by their past," she reassured me. "Everyone makes mistakes, but everyone can also learn from them. Being wise doesn't mean never being wrong; being wealthy doesn't mean never experiencing poverty or financial struggles; and even being successful doesn't mean never failing."

"Hope is the key to turning things around. Hope is the process of anticipating what lies ahead in life. Holding on to hope is an attitude of realistic optimism, not fantasy. If we have faith and entrust everything in our lives to God, He will make everything beautiful and good according to His will," she concluded.

I sighed. "Fine. I think I'm ready to listen to your advice—especially since you've already brought God up in the conversation," I said begrudgingly. I was understandably feeling a bit judged and blamed.

"Could we please stop with the complaining? We orangutans already have enough issues to deal with. Let's focus our efforts on resolving them so that there's hope for orangutans to continue living in the forest in the future.

So, the first thing you need to focus on is this: learn from nature. Nature is already rich in examples of balance and tolerance. This is why it is natural for us to view the Earth as an embodiment of a mother—a mother who is forgiving, understanding, yet full of hope for her children, guiding them with that hope. It reminds me of what Ibn Arabi, a Middle Eastern philosopher, once said: 'Look at all of creation—especially humanity—with goodwill: accept, acknowledge, forgive, serve, and love.' Make this your character, and let these virtues shape your disposition and how you relate to the world. This is why we all truly need to learn from nature," she said wisely.

"Wow, that is indeed good advice. But how can *we* learn from nature? It's not easy to understand it, let alone learn from it," I replied.

"Have you ever heard of Confucius's advice on life?" she asked, choosing not to answer directly. "He once said: 'I hear and I forget. I see and I remember. I do and I understand.' Simply put, take action—do it so you can understand."

I exclaimed, "Oh! That reminds me of advice from another Middle Eastern philosopher, Abu Hamid al-Ghazali. He said, 'Live among people as though you were a fruit-bearing tree. Even if people throw stones at it, the tree still repays them with fruits.'"

"Now that's smart! So, don't despair and don't blame others. Instead, learn from nature and share goodness with every one of His creations. However, kindness requires consistency in action; without it, it becomes nothing more than a fleeting hope," she replied, still clinging to the tree.

As she began to move away, she added, "Back to the topic of orangutans who are displaced from their natural habitat and confined to enclosures—we need to be returned to our rightful home: the forest." She spoke resolutely. "Will humans take immediate action to help? Not all of them. Many will respond with: 'Later. We'll help when we have the money.' But the point isn't about helping later. What matters is what you can do right now."

"Showing commitment through action is essential because it fosters hope. And it is hope that gives us resilience, allowing us to move forward," Lesley concluded with finality. "'Hope is the dream of an awakened man,' according to Aristotle, the Greek philosopher."

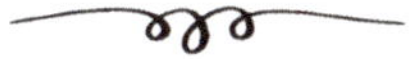

We have decided to save the orangutans and their habitat. But this dream can only be realized through action—through conservation. Conservation is not just a cause; it's a movement that requires tangible efforts. The goals of conservation can't be accomplished solely through seminars and meetings; real, concrete actions are essential.

We all have brains to think, legs to walk, and the ability to envision where we want to go. So let's do what we can, wherever we are, with the resources we have at hand. After all, every great journey begins with a single step, and even a small light can guide you through the darkness.

This means that every effort in support of orangutan conservation, no matter how small, will have a significant impact on both the orangutans and their habitat. There is no need to prioritize one role over another, as each is important. Just like in an orchestra, there can be no symphony unless every musician plays their part. So, there is still hope for the orangutans.

The Greek philosopher Thales once reminded us, "Hope is the only good that is common to all men. Those who have nothing else still possess hope." Let us hold on to that hope and continue our efforts.

To this day, I still remember what my father once told me when I I hesitated to reprimand someone for wrongdoing: "God will hold you accountable for the mistakes of others that you could have prevented or reminded them about, but didn't." People are accountable for the good they fail to do, even when they have the chance. So let's take action. By working together, we can bring hope to the forest and orangutans in Indonesia. As Bertrand Russell once said, "The only thing that will redeem humanity is cooperation."

Then I faintly heard Lesley, my orangutan friend, whisper, "'*Potius sero quam nunquam*,'—it is better late than never."

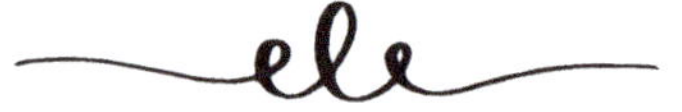

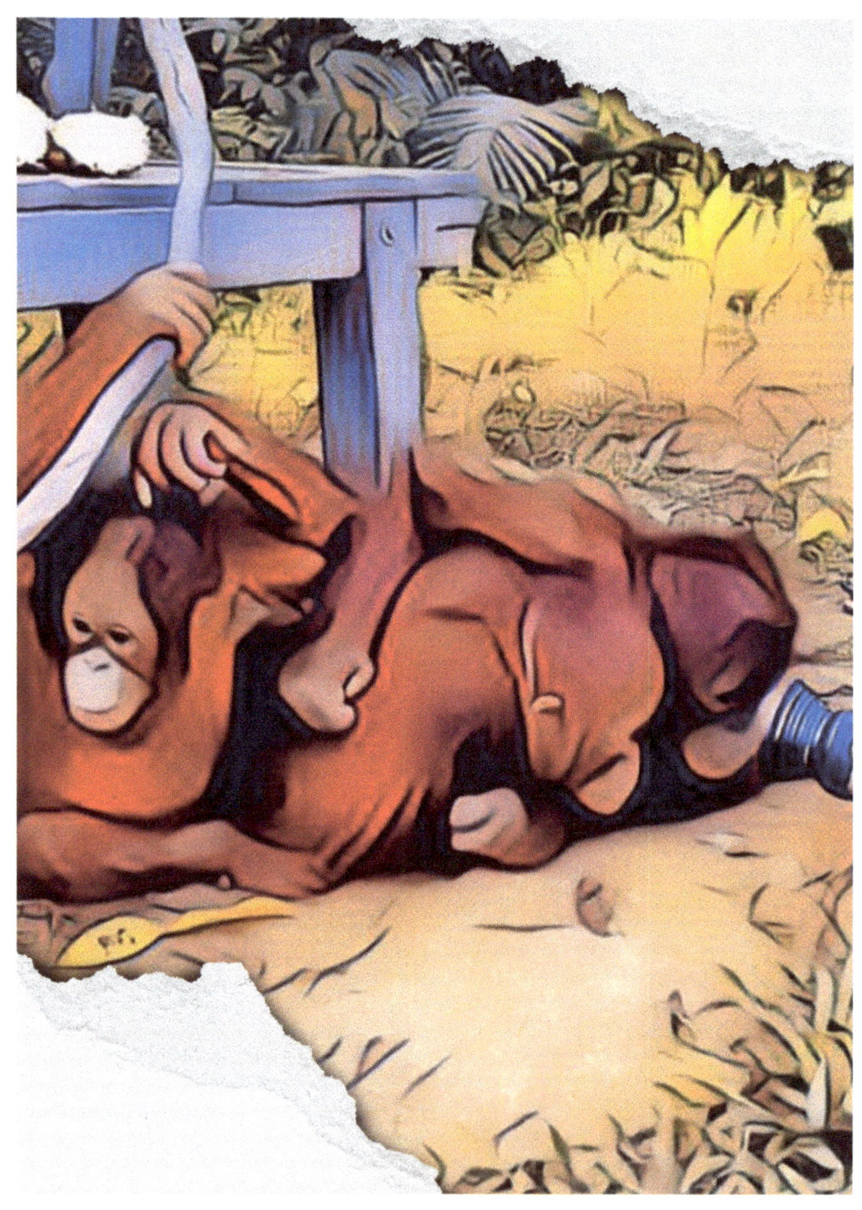

*"Madness is the inability to communicate
what is in the mind"*

- Paulo Coelho, the Brazilian novelist

Chapter 16

Public Communication in Orangutan Conservation

Over a decade ago, a headhunter took me to visit the Borneo Orangutan Survival Foundation (BOSF). I had just one word to sum up my impression: "WOW." BOSF's conservation efforts to rehabilitate orangutans were truly extraordinary. Despite my years of experience in conservation, what I saw there left me in awe. It turned out there was a local Indonesian NGO (Non-Governmental Organization) whose quality was on par with international organizations! However, since internet connectivity was scarce at the time, few people were aware of the work being done by this organization. What a pity.

While I was contemplating near the gates of the rehabilitation center in Nyaru Menteng, Central Kalimantan, I suddenly spotted an orangutan swinging from a tree. A staff member who was monitoring the orangutan commented, "That orangutan is skipping Forest School." Can you believe it? An orangutan playing truant! I chuckled at his remark.

I watched as the orangutan swung playfully from a tree branch. The orangutan, in turn, was watching me. I didn't know how long that moment lasted—time seemed to disappear. When I regained my focus, there was just me and that orangutan, so we greeted each other.

"Hey, why are you sitting in the corner with a furrowed brow?" the school-skipping orangutan asked.

"Furrowed brow? Wow, I didn't expect you to be able to read my face," I replied cheerfully, pleasantly surprised.

"Hahaha... you must have forgotten. There's only a slight difference between our DNAs, you know," he said, swinging closer to where I was sitting. The morning sunlight gently filtered through the gaps in the leaves, turning the orangutan's fur golden brown. It was so beautiful.

"I appreciate your concern, my friend. I'm feeling perplexed. Or, to be more precise, I feel that something is not quite right with the current situation. I see the wonderful work being done by these people here to care for orangutans, but due to a lack of information sharing, the general public remains unaware of it," I tried to explain my thoughts to the orangutan.

"As someone who has spent years working in conservation, you shouldn't be bothered, my friend. Aren't you conservationists always proud of the phrase, "The world of conservation is a silent path, far from the glitter of the news?" Hahaha! Isn't taking concrete action the source of your pride, drive, and fulfillment in orangutan conservation?

As the primary actors in conservation, the technical aspects of working onsite with orangutans alone may not be enough for others to understand the conservation efforts you're making, as it is fieldwork. To achieve this, you need to communicate your work to the public," he said.

"It's just that, until recently, conservation experts may have overlooked the fact that public communication is crucial to the success of wildlife conservation efforts. While wildlife conservation is often associated with the fields of biology and other exact sciences, the solution ultimately lies with human involvement. Humans are both the resource and the solution to overcoming the challenges in conservation. If the human factor is ignored, there will never be an end to the work in the field," explained my orangutan friend.

"That is true. Humans can play both roles: they can be destroyers of nature, but they can also be its protectors," I muttered quietly, feeling ashamed to acknowledge that we humans are a source of the problem.

"Exactly! That's the purpose of public communication and why it is important in conservation work. So, it's not just about natural sciences and social sciences, my friend; it's about how changes in human behavior must absolutely happen. Otherwise, on-the-ground conservation efforts will become a never-ending, vicious circle."

"What do you mean?" I asked, quite astonished by his explanation.

"Here's what I mean. You must be in dire need of public awareness, right? This can only be achieved if public communication and conservation form a complete circle—starting with communication: which involves gathering ideas, sharing thoughts, broadcasting messages, and delivering information. Communication is considered successful only when the message sent by the sender is understood by the recipient, and leads to the expected impact or change (as intended by the message maker).

In this context, whose expectations are we discussing? Those of the conservationists working on the ground. And who can effectively convey this message? The communication experts. Good communication should have an impact on the target audience. For example, a high level of community awareness and investment in conservation efforts is driven by effective promotion and advocacy initiatives.

Let's consider an example from the business world. One of the primary goals of promotion and communication is to raise awareness of the importance of a brand or product. Why is this important? Because greater awareness increases the target consumers' ability to recognize or remember a product, including its name, image, logo, and specific slogans used in its promotion. This product recognition and recall significantly influence consumers' purchasing decisions.

The same holds true in the field of conservation. Communication is considered successful when it raises public awareness and helps people understand the importance of supporting conservation efforts. It seems simple, but it's not easy," said the orangutan.

"Wait a minute, how do you know the ins and outs of business, anyway? Didn't you even skip school today?" I asked, chuckling. I found it hard to believe that this orangutan was as smart as he appeared.

"Are you just curious, or do you really want to know? Oh, but you'll just be nosy if I tell you. Hahaha..." He teased, laughing.

"Hahaha, you are indeed one clever orangutan. Okay, let's return to our discussion. So, does this mean that business logic should be applied to conservation work?" I asked, genuinely interested this time.

"The bottom line is simple, my friend. How can the public understand the efforts of conservationists and their goals when they are not given any information? This reminds me of what Paulo Coelho, the Brazilian novelist, once said, 'Madness is the inability to communicate what is in the mind.' In your case, it means that those of you who work in conservation often struggle to explain the purpose of your work, and some even take pride in being labeled 'crazy'. What is the point of your pride if you can't convey the significance of your work in a way that helps achieve the goals you're striving for, leading towards a better future?"

"Wait, how did you know about Paulo Coelho?" I asked, surprised.

"Oh, you! Never mind that. This was something I overheard yesterday when I eavesdropped on the orangutan foster mothers' conversations as they opened our cages early in the morning so we could go to school."

"Wow, eavesdropping. Okay, okay. But, you're really cool," I said sincerely, laughing in amusement. "Anyway, let's get back to the topic. I agree with you. Conservation work should be communicated to the public—not in complicated scientific language, but in a way that is easy to understand. After all, effective communication has the potential to broaden minds and influence policies, leading to changes in human behavior, and ultimately attracting resources and funding." I concluded.

"Well done! Now you've finally grasped the concept. This is a complex job with several influencing factors that make communication in conservation both an opportunity and a challenge," he said.

"Let's look at a few of them. <u>First</u>: conservation efforts for wildlife species often seem invisible when viewed from the human perspective. It is very difficult to imagine how the lives of orangutans in the forest could impact human lives. Unfortunately, to address this disconnect, conservationists often choose to highlight the suffering of these animals caused by human actions in their communication.

Inadvertently, this approach forces the public to choose between humans and animals, and most of the time, it is the animals who lose. Therefore, it is crucial to adopt a multidisciplinary leap in thinking when framing messages about wildlife conservation—one that will ideally resonate with society's emotions. Shifting public opinion to favor conservation is essential to ensure the survival of orangutans, rather than relying solely on sympathy to evoke pity," he explained.

"<u>Secondly</u>, the inability or failure of conservationists to effectively communicate the outcomes of their multidisciplinary fieldwork can lead to various interpretations, and often distortions, of information. If this happens, then it's true what Paulo Coelho said: this is a new madness," he reflected, thoughtfully.

My orangutan friend's explanation was simple and insightful. I felt like I was back in university, listening to marketing strategy and business communication lectures.

I continued, "Then this means communication specialists are better suited to explaining conservation issues so that more people can understand what conservationists are currently working on and what they have accomplished in the field," I added.

"Well, not always, although there are some cases like that," he calmly replied, like a lecturer answering a question from a new student.

He then continued his explanation: "Conservationists should definitely write about their work in scientific journals to demonstrate that conservation is based on science, not feelings. Unfortunately, though, the language used in these journals is often not one easily understood by the general public. Therefore, conservationists working on the ground, as well as those involved in species conservation, like orangutans, must improve their communication skills so they can explain their work in a way that is easy to understand, without losing its scientific essence."

"So, does this mean that communication could also be used as a tool for negotiating with policymakers, garnering public and donor support, and providing timely information to reporters or journalists, rather than just presenting information?" I asked.

"Well, that is the direction conservation communication should take. Instead of merely discussing normative issues (regular information and on-the-ground reports), it must also convey something of value, so the conservation message can be delivered effectively and on target."

"Wow, that just means we need to learn more about how to effectively share our lives and work in conservation so we can gain support and implement solutions to the problems we face," I replied in a soft voice.

"There is no reason to doubt the efforts your peers in the organization have undertaken or are currently implementing. However, when it comes to communicating these efforts, there is only one effective way to learn. Do it through action, rather than waiting for someone to provide a thick manual to instruct you."

After finishing his sentence, the orangutan darted away from me with natural agility. When I shouted and asked where he was going, he replied that he was going to catch up with his friends at Forest School.

My lively conversation with the orangutan showed me that the connection between wildlife conservation and communications is now very close—something unimaginable in the early 1980s. At the time, conservation approaches were still compartmentalized. Communication was primarily associated with the social sciences and used as a means to engage with people, while conservation was linked to technical fieldwork and the exact sciences. Unbeknownst to us, these two fields have since converged at an invisible intersection.

The success of species conservation, particularly for orangutans, is not solely measured by the increase in population size. There is another often overlooked yet crucial aspect: opening the eyes, hearts, and minds of humans to new horizons and knowledge about conservation. This awareness helps people understand that, as long as they inhabit this planet, they must be part of the solution, not the creators of problems.

Since good intentions for wildlife protection aren't always obvious, let's change our behaviors and attitudes so that everyone develops the awareness and understanding to turn these intentions into meaningful action. That is our hope!

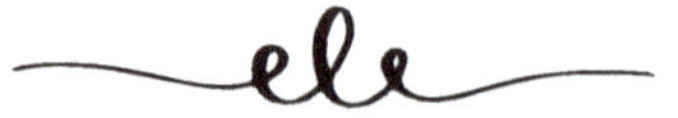

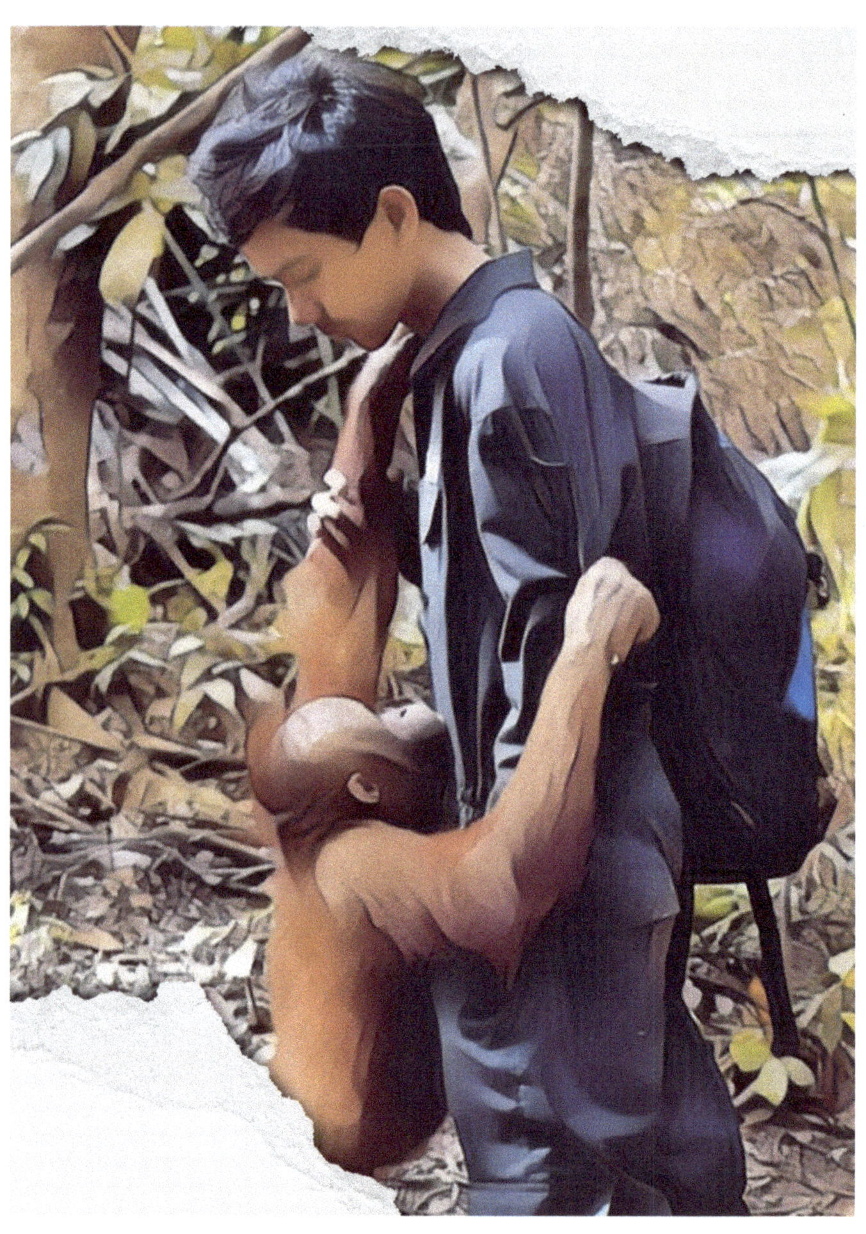

Only when the last tree has been cut down,
only when the last river has been poisoned,
only when the last fish has been caught,
will we realize that
we cannot eat the moneyin our hands!

- a Native American proverb -

Chapter 17

We Need Oxygen, But Its Natural Producer is Destroyed

My brow furrowed when one of the media outlets reported that the demand for medical oxygen in Indonesia was expected to rise to 1,700 metric tons per day as the number of positive COVID-19 cases increased. In addition, 4,700 oxygen concentrators were needed to meet this demand, and the Indonesian government even planned to import oxygen. Wow, Indonesia, considered the "lungs of the world," was forced to import oxygen. We have forests, yet we still have to purchase oxygen. How astonishing!

Around the world, many people seemed shocked when they learned that, due to the COVID-19 outbreak, oxygen became a luxury item. Should we thank COVID-19 for making us aware of how kind and generous nature—a gift from God—has been to humanity? Are we aware of our indifference to the generosity of nature and all the animals that play a role in providing environmental services?

I was reminded of Sepang, one of my orangutan friends who now lives in the forests of Bukit Baka Bukit Raya National Park in Central Kalimantan. He was released on World Conservation Day in 2018.

That day, while I sat contemplating in my home office, remembering the peaceful respite I had by the riverbank after Sepang's release, he appeared in my mind, and I had an exciting imaginary conversation with him.

"How are you, Sepang? You are now free and living in the forest with other orangutans. You must be so happy."

"Of course, we are happy because we have returned home. We are also happy because now we can carry out our *fitrah*—our inherent, true nature—in keeping with the purpose for which God created us. We can also fulfill our duties as mandated by the Creator. Hahaha, I think you understand this very well, my friend. We were created to live freely in the forest, not confined in a cage. And by being in the forest, we can play our part in supporting human life."

"Wait, what do you mean by that? Why are you emphasizing your *fitrah* (inherent nature) and your role in relation to humans?" I asked with great curiosity.

"Allow me to explain," he said. "Do you realize that when we orangutans are in the forest, we serve as gardeners for the forest? By dispersing the seeds from the food we eat, those seeds grow into a variety of trees, which in turn help maintain the biodiversity that improves the health of the forest. Don't forget that a healthy forest provides clean water, clean air (especially oxygen, which is vital to all living things), timber, and non-timber forest products. And what I've mentioned are just a few of the benefits."

"Ah, I see now. Thanks," I said, slightly dismissively.

"You don't seem sincere with your gratitude! Hahaha..." he remarked, laughing at my response. He then continued the conversation by asking, "By the way, how are you dealing with the COVID-19 pandemic right now? The wind and the rain brought the news to us in the forest."

"Since the COVID-19 pandemic is worsening, the situation has become more severe. People are confined and restricted from leaving their homes. We are in semi-lockdown, especially since the emergency public activity restriction policy (PPKM Darurat, in Indonesian) is in place. Hospitals are full, and the demand for oxygen is increasing as more people contract COVID-19. Many residents are angry because it's been over a year since their mobility was restricted. Many people cannot work and have lost their income, but all the costs—and, as a result, all expenses—have increased. The country is close to bankruptcy," I said in a barely audible voice. The circumstances have also impacted our day-to-day work in the field.

"Hmm... do you think that's karma or a lack of gratitude?" he said, teasing me. Then his expression turned serious. He rubbed his chin while nodding. His gaze was fixed on me— his conversation partner, who probably looked naive in his eyes.

"Uhm, why do you sound sarcastic, my friend?" I asked uneasily, my voice rising in pitch.

"I'm not, actually. I'm just perplexed by you humans, who are supposed to be the smartest. Now please listen and don't interrupt. Think with your heart... with your heart! Not your brain, okay? You humans, who have only been restricted for less than two years, are already extremely frustrated. Now, compare that to my friends at the Rehabilitation Centre. We are confined because of human actions, and not just for a year or two, but for many years. Yet, all you humans say about what we endure is, 'Oh, you poor thing,' but you hardly do anything.

Then, suddenly, humans worldwide are affected by the COVID-19 pandemic, caused by a virus that originated from wildlife in the forest. But the truth is, you took that wildlife from the forest and turned it into food—even though these animals are never meant for your consumption! And then there's the forest we have planted and cared for, alongside other wildlife. You cut it down for the sake of making money! Too often, you humans believe that if you have money, you can buy anything. Now that oxygen is scarce, can you breathe in your money?" he scoffed derisively.

He then went on to say, "There is a Native American proverb that says: 'Only when the last tree has been cut down, only when the last river has been poisoned, only when the last fish has been caught, will we realize that we cannot eat the money in our hands!' Thus, humanity's decision to profit from nature at the expense of destroying it is unwise. So, in my opinion, humans are severely lacking in gratitude!"

"What do you mean? Why do you say that humans are ungrateful?" I replied, my voice rising again, as I really disliked what Sepang was implying. While there was nothing wrong with his explanation, sometimes admitting the truth hurts.

"You don't need to raise your voice like that. Hahaha..." he responded with a laugh as if to point out how naive and foolish we humans are.

Then he continued his explanation, "Now, why do I say humans are ungrateful? Imagine this: each minute, the average human adult breathes in about 7-8 liters of air. If we calculate that, in a single day, a human being inhales approximately 11,000 liters of air. Keep in mind, these numbers account for the air used during normal, non-vigorous activity. However, if an individual engages in more frequent or more strenuous activities, the amount of air inhaled on that day could rise to 12,000 liters.

Of the 11,000 liters of air we breathe each day, about 20% is oxygen. This means that a human inhales approximately 2,200 liters of oxygen per day. Using this figure (2,200 liters) and the market price of oxygen, which is Rp. 15,000 per liter, we can calculate the value of the oxygen we breathe each day. The result, in Indonesian Rupiah (IDR), is Rp. 33,000,000. However, due to COVID-19, there has been a high demand for oxygen, and the price per liter has increased by Rp. 5,000, bringing the total cost to Rp. 44,000,000. Keep in mind that this price is for just one person and does not include the cost of tubes and regulators.

Now, think about how many people there are around the world. Is it wrong for us orangutans to say that humans are ungrateful? Nature has given you a bonus worth around 30 million rupiahs every day, for free, in the form of oxygen. And that's not even counting the other benefits you receive for free.

Think about that Native American proverb again. Shouldn't both humans and wildlife always be grateful for the blessings and miracles we receive from God? Isn't He wonderful to both you and me? Doesn't the human Scripture say, "Give thanks in all circumstances..."?

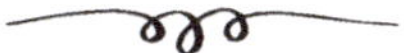

My brow furrowed even more as I reflected on my conversation with Sepang, the orangutan. He reminded me of how rich my country, Indonesia, truly is. Even when we overlook the services that nature and wildlife provide, it turns out that, thanks to the environmental services provided by the forest, we humans have been able to live well from the very beginning.

Due to the COVID-19 pandemic, we finally realized our need for precious oxygen, but our disregard for the environment has destroyed nature, which has freely provided us with it. So, yes, the orangutan is right. We need oxygen, but we destroy their forest homes, which provide us with that oxygen!

As I sat pondering in the corner of my home office, under the movement restrictions imposed by the pandemic, I faintly heard an orangutan say, "Return us to the forest and protect our homes, and you will receive all the benefits for free. By helping us orangutans stay in the forest, you are also helping yourself."

Softly, I could also hear the melody of the wind and the river water singing, "The life we should lead must be one of gratitude…"

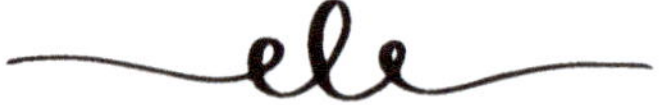

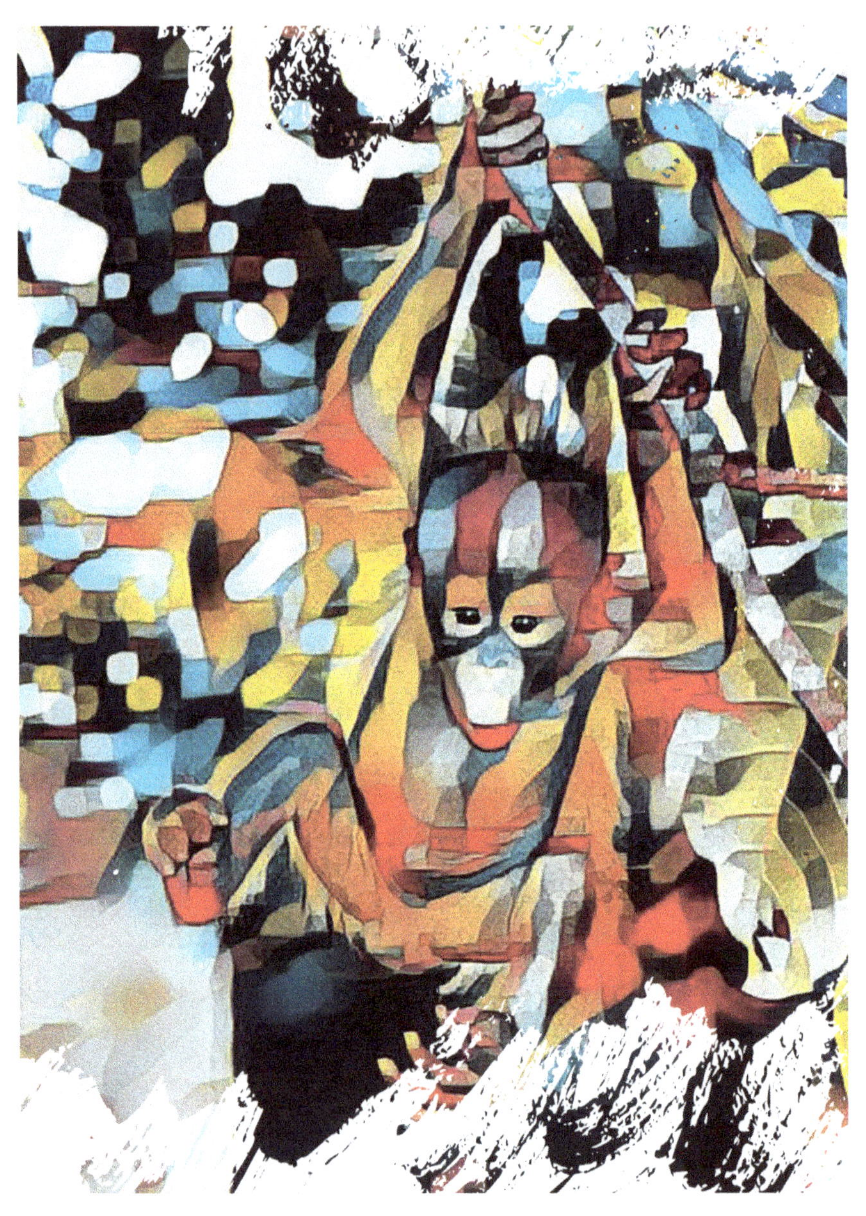

"Laborare est orare!"

- Your work is your prayer!

Easy to Slip Into, Tough to Shake Off

One afternoon, when the weather was far from welcoming, I thought of one of my orangutan friends at the BOSF (Borneo Orangutan Survival Foundation) Rehabilitation Center in Kalimantan. As I sat in contemplation, the cold atmosphere and heavy rain seemed to connect my mind with that of my orangutan friend. We soon became immersed in a warm conversation, despite the unfriendly weather that accompanied our chat. Thankfully, the cacophony of rain, wind, and lightning—which seemed unwilling to make peace—could not interrupt our dialogue.

My orangutan friend had just returned from Forest School and was sitting in his enclosure, waiting for nightfall when I greeted him.

"Hello, my friend," I said. "How was your day at Forest School?"

"I'm doing well, and I want to thank you for saving us from those who thought they rescued us out of love," he replied. "They kept us in cages in their homes, never considering how we might have ended up there."

I was taken aback. What happened? Why wasn't he answering my question? Instead, he was complaining about his past life in captivity, even though today he was re-learning how to be a true orangutan from us humans, not from his mother.

"You don't need to dwell on that old wound, my friend," I said cautiously. "You've already begun learning the skills that will prepare you for your return to the forest, haven't you?"

The orangutan remained quiet. He moved to the corner of his enclosure, his fingers gripping the bars, and his gaze seemed to drift to a place far, far away.

I fell silent, too. I thought to myself, "Did my words hurt him? Does he still carry some inner wounds? Or have I made him so emotionally uncomfortable that he now sees me as just another human?"

"Hey, why are you so quiet?" I said gently, breaking the silence.

"I'm not. I was just thinking and trying to understand your thoughts," he replied.

"I'm sorry if I said something wrong," I said in a low tone, afraid of hurting his feelings.

"It's not a matter of right or wrong, you know. Sometimes, a particular viewpoint can make what's wrong seem right. It's just that—why am I not allowed to process my inner wounds, like when humans killed my mother and seized me from her embrace?" I saw clear drops of water fall from the corner of his eyes.

"I'm truly sorry. What's going through your mind right now?" I asked.

"I can't help but feel pity for all of you here at this Rehabilitation Centre. You're desperately scrambling to find donors so we can return to our home in the forest. Think about it. If you want to protect us from extinction and ensure our survival at a low cost, shouldn't you just let the forest remain as it is and allow us to care for it and be its stewards? Preserving us and protecting the forest must go hand in hand. In captivity, our role is no different from that of any other caged animal—on display for your own glorification." My friend's voice was firm, even though he conveyed his thoughts in a soft, flat tone.

"You're right. It's just that maintaining the forest and letting you remain in it aren't as simple as it sounds," I said defensively.

"Hahaha... that means if you truly want it, it can be done. It's not an impossibility. We orangutans think that you humans are simply being oblivious. Isn't it true that when one door to happiness closes, another opens? The problem is that you focus too long on the closed door. You are so preoccupied with finding answers about why that door has closed that you fail to notice other doors that are open. Because of that, you miss out on other opportunities that God has provided for you. Remember, you will never fail until you stop trying."

"That's true," I said, feeling chastised. "But, training and releasing you back to the wild is also not easy, either," I argued.

"Let's consider my experience and that of my fellow orangutans in any rehabilitation center," he said, looking at me intently. "Look how easily you humans take us away from our roots and life in the forest, kill our orangutan mothers, and force us, orangutan children, to be treated like human children or as pets!"

Then he continued, "Thus, Friedrich Nietzsche, a German philosopher who lived from 1844 to 1900, was not mistaken when he said: 'Man is the cruelest animal.' Because of this, orangutan children have become domesticated and are ill-equipped to return to their home in the forest. Then, everyone at the rehabilitation centre must struggle for years to teach us how to live as orangutans. It is all too easy for us to forget God's command about the reason we orangutans were created in the forest. Just as it is easy for you to fall into bad habits, even though God has given us His word on what we can and cannot do."

"Yes, it's easy to slip into and tough to shake off," I said in a barely audible voice.

"Hahaha, that's your sin, humans!" the orangutan said sardonically, even as he laughed.

"Wait a minute. Why are we talking about sins now?!" I said, unwilling to accept his words.

"All humans are aware of how easy it is to commit sin and how difficult it is to break bad habits. Why does that happen? Because humans are composed of both spirit and flesh. The spirit is willing, but the flesh is weak. Humans are beings of spirit, desiring to do what is virtuous—while also beings of flesh, making them susceptible to the temptations of their earthly nature. Do you understand? If not, let me explain," he said.

"Humans have a spiritual life in which they can commune and have fellowship with God—an intimate and personal relationship with the Creator. On the other hand, because humans are also creatures of flesh who have fallen into sin (by transgressing divine law), they are often swayed by the nature of sin. It is their moral wrongdoing that causes them to deviate from God's will. The desire of the flesh—the human ego—often puts humans at odds with God, causing them to forget His commands, such as maintaining the integrity of His creation," he expounded thoughtfully.

Then he looked at me intently. "Now let me ask you this: how can humans claim to love God, yet destroy what He has created? There's no point to your lives if you devote only one day a week to worshiping God, while the rest of the time you live in a way that denies Him. So, don't neglect or live contrary to God's teachings. Remember, my friend, your attitude and behavior are also your prayers to the Creator," the orangutan reminded me.

The rain continued to fall heavily, and the wind howled fiercely. I faintly heard the orangutan's voice: "Weakness is no excuse for sin. Never justify your sinful actions with the saying, 'The spirit is willing, but the flesh is weak.' God will hold you accountable if you choose to remain silent when you know someone is committing wrongdoing and allow them to continue in their ways until the end of their life. As the saying goes, 'Labourare est orare!'—your work is your prayer! So, pray for your work and do what you pray for."

I became contemplative for a while after hearing everything he said. It hit me hard and deep.

We humans have so easily uprooted orangutans from their homes and natural habitats. Sadly, we have become so accustomed to such inconsiderate, even callous behaviors—behaviors that God disapproves of—that we casually continue them, even normalizing them without hesitation. It's tragic.

I have always considered humans to be fairly smart and wise, but the truth is, we are better at holding on to bad behaviors and have found it difficult to let go of them in order to change for the better. The same applies to orangutan conservation efforts. The unfortunate reality is that, as long as we remain unwilling to change, wildlife will always be in trouble.

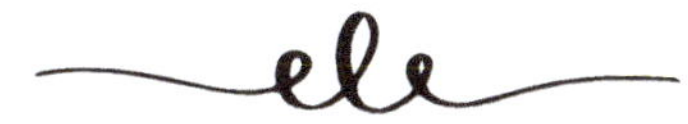

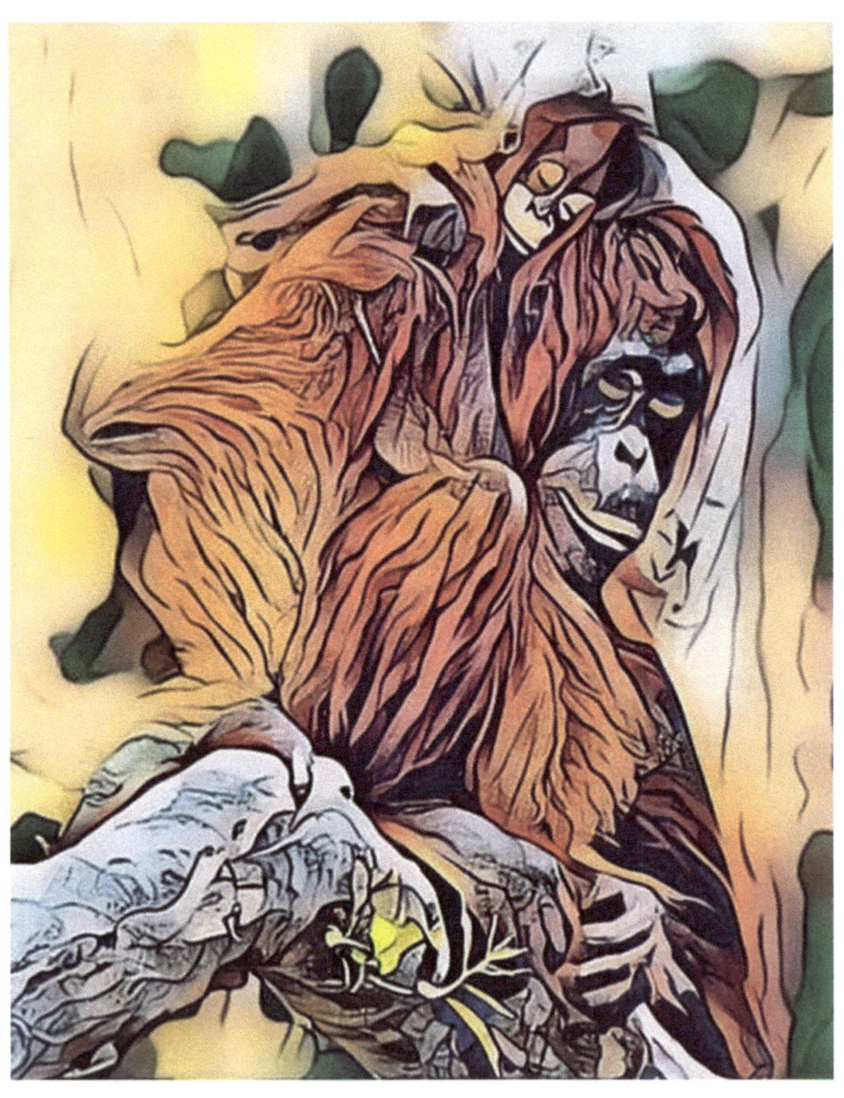

*"The human attitude of favoring their own species,
while exploiting or harming other species
is another form of racism"*

- Richard Ryder, 1970

Chapter 19

Lecture by Orangutan Mother

One day, after completing all the tasks involved in an orangutan release, we rested at the "post-release monitoring" camp. I decided to visit the riverbank to enjoy the shade of the trees and the soothing song of the river. Isn't it amazing how the silence of the forest and the sounds of nature can replenish our energy?

As I sat lost in thought, with memories of the orangutans and the release work coursing through my mind, I noticed an orangutan swinging from a branch not far from where I was sitting, contemplating. She was a female orangutan who had been freed only a few years earlier, and she was carrying her baby, born in the forest. Our eyes met, and I smiled at the sight of her holding her baby. Although we remained physically apart; it felt as though we were mentally connected. Soon after, we quickly entered into an imaginary dialogue.

"Hey, what are you thinking about? You're tired, huh?" The orangutan mother greeted me with a warm voice and friendly smile.

"Tired? Yes, of course, *bu*. Our journey, both by land and river, was quite tiring. Even though we spent hours just sitting, we were happy. The fatigue was worth it when we saw our friend—and your friend—safe and free in his home in the forest," I explained.

I intentionally addressed her with the honorific term "ibu" (Madam) or its shorter form "bu" (Ma'am) as a sign of respect for her—as a female orangutan created by God, who had successfully mated and given birth in the forest.

"Is the release process still the same as when I was set free? Do you still need to involve so many people?" she asked with curiosity.

"As usual, *bu*. You know that the work involved, from rehabilitation to release, is both complex and challenging—it can't be done by just one or two people."

The orangutan gave a small smile as she gently stroked her baby. It seemed as though she was whispering something—perhaps answering a question from her young, forest-born child, who was likely seeing humans for the first time.

"Why are you smiling like that, *bu*?" I asked, my voice tinged with anxiety. "Did you notice something unusual? Didn't you go through the same release process?"

"Oh, come on now. Don't be so quick to take offense. I'm smiling because I'm grateful to be in the forest. On the other hand, I'm also smiling wryly when I think back on your human folly—humans who always claim to be the smartest creatures," she chided.

"Well, can you tell me why you smile like that at us, especially when we go to the trouble of bringing your orangutan friends back to the forest?" I asked the orangutan mother, slightly exasperated.

"Okay, listen, and pay attention. But refrain from doing what you did in college, where you kept your eyes on the lecturer while your mind wandered elsewhere. Hahaha..." she said, teasing me.

"Huh? Alas! I'm busted. Hahaha... Alright, fine. Come on, *Ibu*, please tell me and enlighten me," I pleaded eagerly.

"When I was a child, I was torn from my mother and forced to witness her death. You know, taking a baby orangutan from its mother also means taking the mother's life—and in my case, depriving me of a mother. After that, I was raised by humans and passed around from one family to another. They tried to love me, treating me like one of their own. I was dressed, carried, and fed human food. Unfortunately, they never considered, let alone questioned, whether that was what I truly needed and wanted," she reminisced, her voice tinged with sorrow.

"During my time with humans, I kept asking myself, 'How could they have had the heart to kill my mother and forcibly take me from her?'" she said, contemplatively.

"It wasn't until I lived in the forest and had my own baby that I finally understood the extent of human greed. It's no wonder Gandhi once said, 'The world has enough for all His creations, but not enough for two people's greed!'"

"That's fascinating, *bu*. You are as wise as a philosopher," I said, trying to be playful, hoping to lighten the mood and make the conversation more relaxed. But the orangutan mother seemed uninterested in my jest and continued with her story.

"I realized that, as a mother, I would never willingly leave my child, let alone hand him over to humans. So, any human who claims to have found an orangutan child abandoned by its mother is telling the saddest, most outrageous lie! Now I understand why my mother was killed when the poachers came for me. It was because the captivating gaze of an orangutan child—my gaze—made anyone fall in love with it. I came to this realization only after I gave birth," she explained.

"The eyes of a baby orangutan—indeed, the eyes of all our children—are both a blessing and a curse," she said, sighing. "These eyes instantly make many people fall in love with them, yet lead them to harbor malicious intent, making them claim our children as their own."

"Then, without a second thought or any empathy in their hearts, people give our orangutan children what humans usually want, just as they would with their own. But, they forget that orangutan children were created by God for the forest. Humans don't realize they have no right to uproot us orangutans from our *fitrah*—our natural state in which we were created. Humans are not our God!" the orangutan mother exclaimed in frustration. She fell silent, her eyes instantly welling up with tears.

I then commented, trying to calm her down. "Well, we are humans; we are certainly not your God. I understand that you're upset, but there's really no need to be so dramatic, *bu*."

"In that case, what right do you have to determine our lives?" she retorted angrily. "I'll say it again: when you humans take an orangutan child from its mother, you also take away that mother's life. It's so easy for you to do—with just one or two people—and in just a matter of minutes, the life of an orangutan child is completely changed! Just imagine! In the blink of an eye, our lives are turned upside down. You even change our behavior. Not to mention the impact you have on our health, as some of us are forced to live with the diseases that you transmit to us, intentionally or not. Is that what love means to you, humans? Because of diseases brought by humans, many of my kin can no longer return to the forest."

"I am reminded of a wise phrase by Arthur Schopenhauer, translated into Spanish: '*Para ser sinceros: los seres humanos son los diablos de la tierra y los animales las almas atormentadas*,' meaning, 'In truth, humans are the devils of the earth, and animals are the tortured souls.' Do you know who Arthur Schopenhauer was? He was a German philosopher who lived from 1788 to 21 September 1860. He was one of the first to defend non-domestic animals, issuing numerous statements in support of their rights. In his day, he was considered a madman. And yes, just like the way you at BOSF are seen today." Her voice trembled, as though she was holding back both anger and sadness.

"Yes, you're right," I said, feeling proud to be compared to a philosopher, though it was clearly in a sarcastic tone.

"Can I finish my story before you comment?" she asked, exasperated. "This is such a common attitude among you humans—thinking you know what's best for us orangutans. We understand your way of thinking. You feel that by using your human sentiments, you can read our feelings. But, there is still that 3 percent difference in our DNA, so don't impose your feelings and thoughts on us orangutans."

"Okay, okay. Please continue your story, *bu...*" I said quietly, afraid of being scolded again for interrupting her explanation.

"So, it takes just one or two humans, and only five minutes, to kill our mothers and take our children. Then, they bring our orangutan babies into their homes and completely alter their lives! In the forest, before we came into contact with humans, we had no knowledge of tuberculosis (TB)— but you transmitted it to us. As a result, we are forced to spend the rest of our lives in cages. And you humans do this in the name of love and compassion," she said, emphasizing her point.

"Did you know that in the 1970s, Richard Ryder, a writer and animal rights advocate, stated that the human attitude of favoring their own species while exploiting or harming other species is another form of racism? Then, in October 1978, UNESCO issued the Universal Declaration of Animal Rights, which asserts that the fundamental right of wild animals is to live freely in their natural habitat and reproduce. What do you think? Isn't it obvious how harmful humans have been?" she said, insistently.

"What a fascinating lecture this has been. I feel like I'm back in a philosophy class. You've provided some good information, *bu*," I said quietly, feeling just as inspired as I did when I was in university.

"That seems to be a problem with you. Don't you value your local indigenous wisdom? Isn't there a lot of local wisdom in Indonesia that uses nature-based analogies to teach? Take, for example, the proverb of the Minangkabau people of West Sumatra that says, "*Alam takambang menjadi guru*," which translates as: "The vast expanse of nature serves as a teacher." Therefore, learn from nature. Let me continue, so that, for once, we orangutans can be the ones teaching you humans. You're not the only ones who can teach at Forest School, you know. Hahaha... "

"Sorry, but could you keep it brief, *bu*? I'm getting hungry, you see, and when I'm hungry, my brain has trouble absorbing information."

"The point is simple, and I'll repeat it so you can remember it: It doesn't take many people to take an orangutan baby away from its mother. It also doesn't take long to kill the mother. In fact, just one or two people can do it in five minutes. But the result? We orangutans end up stranded in your homes. Then, when crazy people like you at BOSF rescue us from the backyards of the people who keep us, that's when your challenge begins. Rescuing us is not the end of the journey; it's just the beginning. Remember that well," she said, looking at me intently.

"Then, you, at the rehabilitation center, must start training these orangutan children to acquire the skills necessary to live independently in the forest. This requires the effort of many people and at least five years. It's certainly not easy, is it? It's neither easy nor cheap. You'll also have to learn how orangutan mothers teach their young. So, why kill an orangutan mother if you're just going to learn from one later? Hahaha, how foolish!" she said, sarcastically.

She paused, then continued, "The next challenge for the rehabilitation center is to find a suitable forest for release and ensure we can all adapt and become true orangutans. This search will cost a lot of money and require the hard work of many people. And it all started with the actions of a few fools who robbed the lives of orangutan children. Imagine that!"

"I understand now. Thank you for your lessons, *bu*. Live your life, be a true orangutan in the forest, and be happy with your child."

The orangutan mother tightened her hold on her child. She briefly glanced at me, smiled in acknowledgment, and then began to swing from one branch to another with agile movements, carrying her child in her arms. How remarkable!

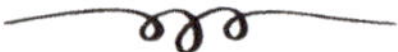

The orangutan mother had long since disappeared from sight, yet I remained seated on the riverbank, my thoughts still wandering to places unknown. The brief lecture I had just received was one I would never have heard in any lecture hall. The message delivered by the orangutan mother was not just for those of us working in orangutan conservation but also for all of us humans—including you and me.

My mind lingered on the words of the German philosopher, Arthur Schopenhauer: *"El hombre ha hecho de la Tierra un infierno para los animales"*—'Man has made the Earth a hell for animals,' he said. His statement made me reflect on how my fellow humans treated other species. Had we truly been so cruel to our fellow creatures? Hadn't God created everything on this earth to be beautiful?

As the breeze gently blew, I heard the orchestra of the river and the leaves singing:

> *How beautiful is the nature created by God,*
> *Animals, birds, fish, plants,*
>
> *And the vast sky, the stars and the moon,*
> *The entire solar system praises the Lord.*

My God watches over the entire universe,
Birds, wildlife have enough to eat.

Teach me, Lord, open my eyes,
To learn from nature and see your wisdom.

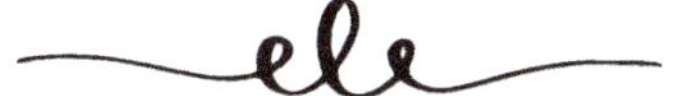

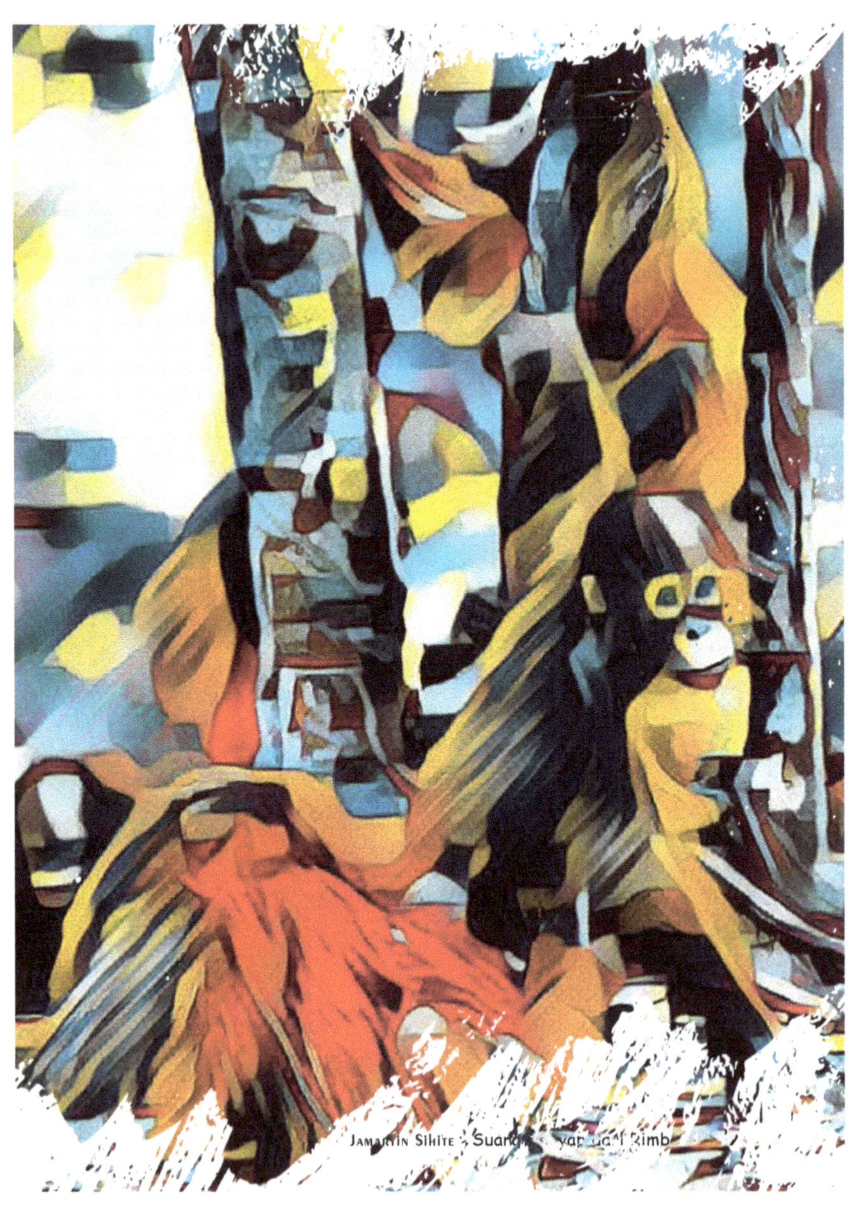
Jamartin Sihite · Suang... yap ... Rimb

Reflecting on coffee, we learned that
black is not dirty, and bitter is not always terrible.
When 'bitter' and 'dirty'
are no longer seen as distressing
—only then can ecotourism
become a viable source of funding for conservation.

Chapter 20

Ecotourism: A Double-edged Sword

I had no idea what prompted me to open an old folder on my computer's hard drive that day. Perhaps it was my growing frustration with the stalled progress of orangutan conservation efforts. As I scrolled through the digital archive, I found myself transfixed by the collection of old images, particularly those that transported me back to the time when my colleagues and I took an impromptu coffee break deep in the jungle of Kalimantan (Indonesian Borneo).

Yes, I still vividly remember the moment we decided, on a whim, that it was time for a coffee break. It happened when the aging rental car we were traveling in—'*Si Tua Seksi*' (The Sexy Old One), as we affectionately called it—broke down in the middle of our journey. That car was the only one we could afford for our forest expedition, and being over twenty years old, she eventually gave out. We had no choice but to get out and wait for her to recover. The only thing we could do in the meantime was take a coffee break.

While resting in the forest, we brewed some coffee. With such a limited supply of ground coffee, we were forced to share the single cup we made.

That moment of togetherness reminded me of the Last Supper before Jesus' crucifixion. We boiled water using a makeshift device, brewed the coffee, sweetened it with palm sugar, stirred it, and then took turns sipping from the same cup—not because a crucifixion was imminent, but because we had so little coffee. Still, this limitation didn't deter us from savoring the coffee together, with gratitude and without complaint. And do you know what it tasted like? So decadent, so delicious! No coffee had ever tasted so good.

When it was my turn, as I savored that cup of sweet black coffee, I became contemplative. Even a simple cup of coffee requires quite a process to produce. You need water, ground coffee, and palm sugar, along with a device for boiling water, a fire, a cup, and a small spoon for stirring. Only after all these steps have been completed can the cup of coffee truly be enjoyed.

Getting good-quality coffee beans also requires a series of careful steps. Every part of the process matters. If the coffee tree is planted, tended, and harvested carelessly, or if the beans are processed improperly, the flavor of the brew will be subpar—or worse, it could cause an upset stomach. If that happens, instead of being a source of enjoyment, the coffee can become a health risk for the drinker.

So, for some people, a cup of coffee is simply that—a drink. But in reality, it's the result of a long journey, full of ups and downs, from the beans to our cup, before we even take that first sip.

Just like making a great-tasting cup of coffee, developing ecotourism requires a careful, thoughtful process. We must not rush it. That doesn't mean we don't prefer it, but we must appreciate each step—just as we take the time to savor the process of creating the aroma and flavor of a good, hot cup of coffee.

Returning to the beginning of this story, as I sat enjoying the fresh air at the edge of the forest, sharing that single cup of coffee with my team, my mind drifted to the orangutans in the rehabilitation center, as well as those already released into the wild. How could orangutans be part of ecotourism? And what kind of ecotourism should that be?

Question after question flooded my mind until Sura—an orangutan we had rescued, who now resided at Borneo Orangutan Survival Foundation's (BOSF) Nyaru Menteng rehabilitation center in Central Kalimantan—appeared to greet me. At that moment, we had an imaginary conversation.

"Hey, are you going to open the orangutan release area to ecotourism?" Without any preamble, Sura asked me a question that perfectly mirrored the thoughts swirling in my mind. Being from Sumatra, I appreciate directness and I'm not one for beating about the bush. But still, his blunt inquiry still startled me.

"Can't I think about the future where we can develop orangutan ecotourism together?" I replied almost spontaneously.

"Ecotourism is not as simple a concept as most people think. It is complex, involving many aspects, principles, and requirements to bring the idea to fruition. Without properly implementing these principles or requirements, the nature-based tourist activities you've proposed cannot be considered ecotourism," he stated flatly. His tone made me realize I had to respond cautiously.

"What concerns you the most about this, Sura?" I asked carefully, worried I might offend him.

"Please don't misunderstand us. We orangutans are not against ecotourism. We understand that humans need nature. Not only does it act as medicine to heal a wounded heart, but it also provides a constant cooling effect. And you humans need that. The forest is also home to various scent-producing plants that can offer a sense of comfort to the body," he said.

"In addition, being in the forest allows people to enjoy the beautiful chorus created by the birds, the water, and the wind—its beauty surpassing even that of world-class orchestral music. Nature's symphony, like the one you experience each time you enter the wilderness, brings peace of mind. Because in nature, all our energies merge into one cohesive symphony. Therefore, you must exercise caution to avoid misconceptions when planning and developing ecotourism. We don't want economic interests to take precedence over ecological concerns," he stated firmly.

"What do you mean by misconceptions, Sura?" I asked, genuinely curious. It seemed like I needed to review my course notes, or perhaps, in this case, let Sura be my mentor, I thought to myself.

"There are several misconceptions about ecotourism. First, not all nature-based tourism qualifies as ecotourism. Many people mistakenly believe that any trip to nature is ecotourism," Sura began. "But, if the tourism program doesn't focus on educating visitors about nature, the local indigenous people and their culture, or managing environmental degradation and loss, it can't be considered ecotourism."

"Second, ecotourism is not cheap, either in cost or quality. While visitors may get sweaty and dirty, their comfort must always be maintained. This is not mass tourism; it is a specialized form of tourism. No matter how great its potential, ecotourism will fail to attract or appeal to tourists unless it is designed, packaged, and marketed strategically and appropriately."

"You still seem to have reservations about ecotourism, my friend," I commented.

"I'll say it again: while we orangutans are not opposed to ecotourism, opening the release area to ecotourism requires caution. Please listen carefully as I explain why. The orangutans released into the wild, including myself, have had previous contact with humans, some of us may have even experienced trauma caused by humans. Despite attending Forest School and living on the pre-release islands at the rehabilitation centers, we can't fully escape the effects of human domestication. If you, the forest managers, or those responsible for protecting the release area, allow ecotourism and tourist visits, you risk exposing us, the recently freed orangutans, to human contact. Unfortunately, this presents a significant risk—not only for us orangutans but also for the visitors."

"A risk? Can you explain that to me in more detail?" I asked him.

"The first concern is the possibility of disease transmission. Anyone entering the release site must be healthy and free from any human diseases. This is a simple requirement for you to manage. The next issue is that visitors might encounter orangutans who haven't fully recovered from domestication or human-induced trauma. This presents a real risk, as these orangutans could potentially endanger visitors. Therefore, for the safety of both humans and orangutans, visitors' activities must be strictly regulated and supervised, ensuring that both humans and orangutans are equally protected."

"I see. So, what is the best way for visitors to enjoy ecotourism in the release forest?" I asked.

"Well, nature has flourished for millions of years, which makes her wise enough to offer you more perspectives on life than even the smartest of people. As a result, nature is the best teacher because every moment spent in her presence is an adventure that undoubtedly offers valuable lessons."

"Wow, there are so many ways to interpret your words, my friend. What are you really trying to tell us?" I said. I expected him to be more concerned about the safety of interactions between visitors and orangutans in areas open to ecotourism, given how much his life had been marred by human cruelty. When poachers snatched him from his mother and then killed her, parts of his fingers were severed by a machete. As a result, all of his fingers are now the same length.

"Orangutans who are accustomed to human presence may assume that all visitors to the forest are our friends," he explained. "But can you see the risk in that? If the visitors have ill intentions, like the poachers I encountered in the past, then our lives would be in danger. The same goes for visitors who aren't familiar with orangutan behavior. If these people haven't been properly educated on how to behave when encountering orangutans—especially those who have suffered trauma at the hands of humans—then the orangutans may feel threatened and could attack."

"Can you imagine what would happen if a human got into a confrontation with an orangutan, whose strength is more than seven times that of an adult human? Dear God! Let those of us who have undergone rehabilitation live out our lives and die in peace before ecotourism is introduced. By then, at least our children and grandchildren will have adapted to life in the wild and will no longer view humans as either their friends or foes. Look deeper into nature, listen more clearly to its full voice, and you will understand everything much better," Sura said, his words slowly fading from my mind.

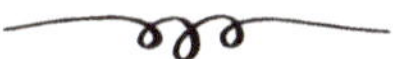

Ecotourism must be presented in a way that appeals to potential tourists. Although it is a niche market, it should not be perceived as cheap and shabby. Perhaps, as Sura the orangutan might say, a cup of coffee can offer valuable insights into ecotourism. So, let us sip our coffee while reflecting on these lessons.

From this cup of coffee, I've learned that black is not always dirty, and bitter is not always terrible. When coffee becomes a true companion, when mornings are no longer a mystery, when bitter and dirty are no longer considered unpleasant, then ecotourism can become a viable source of funding for conservation—even for the future. Prudence, accurate judgment, and balancing economic and environmental interests are key to developing ecotourism. Like a double-edged sword, it is a powerful tool if wielded skillfully, but it can cause harm if mishandled.

Therefore, let us thoughtfully consider and plan for ecotourism, while sipping black coffee and sharpening our skills in handling this double-edged sword.

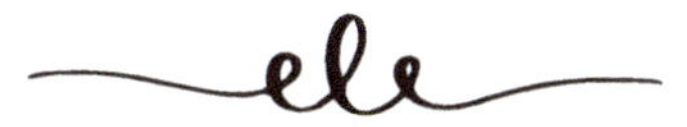

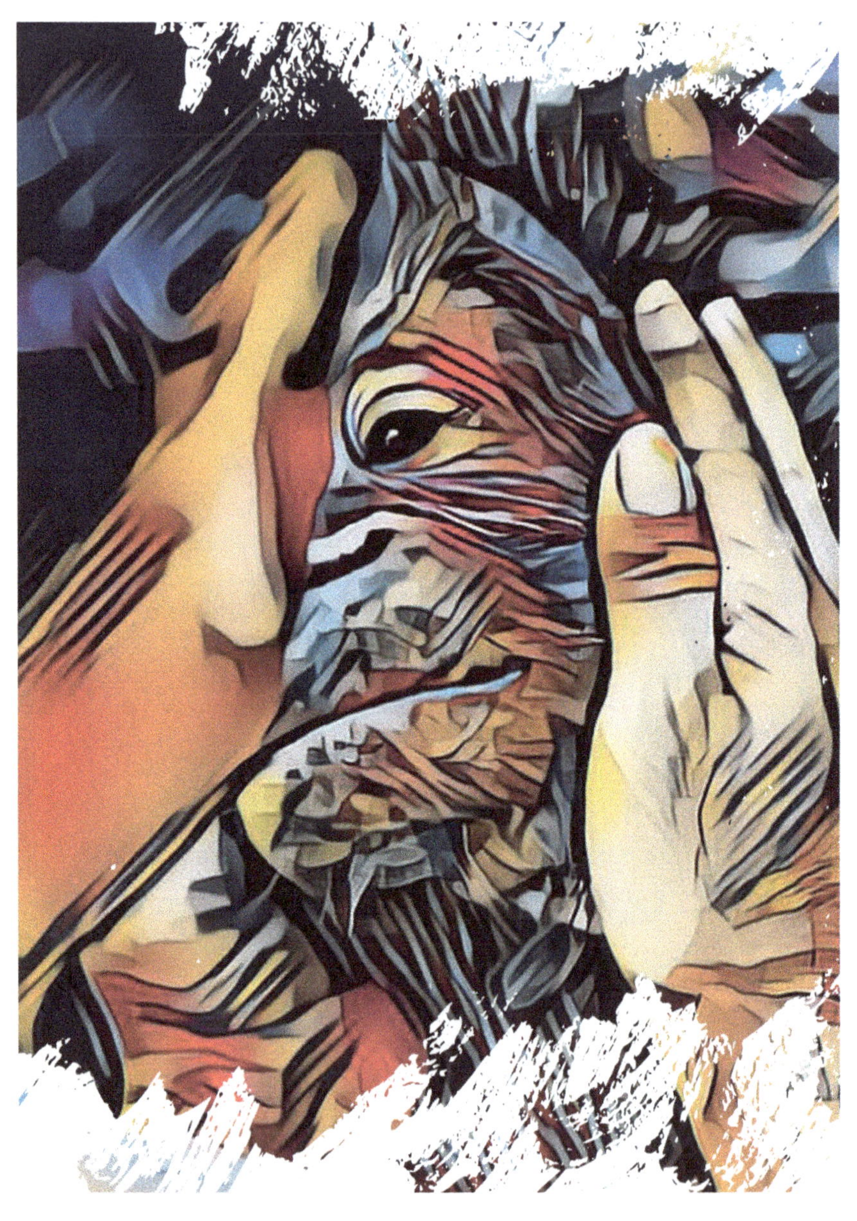

*"Forget the bitterness,
but never forget the lessons.
Disappointments and hurt feelings
have no place in a heart full of gratitude."*

Chapter 21

Going Crazy

One day at the end of the year, the torrential rain and strong winds made the dark afternoon feel more like a year-end party accompanied by a heavy metal rock concert. It's no exaggeration to use the analogy of 'metal' to describe this genre of music, as it often sounds intense or harsh. Yet, behind its fierce image, it's still something that resonates with the heart. Similarly, conservation work must be understood with the heart, not just with the mind.

Despite the pounding beat and the deafening clap of thunder, my mind wandered, recalling my annual trip for orangutan conservation work.

Then I heard, "Hey you, why are you silent when the wind, the rain, and the thunder outside seem to be vying to dominate nature's musical stage?" It was an orangutan I know, greeting me with his voice.

"I'm just reflecting on the journey of our work in conservation. Many things didn't go according to plan or meet our expectations, my friend," I said to the orangutan while wiping away the tears that welled up from disappointment.

"Why are you reacting this way, my friend? Are setbacks and dissatisfaction truly worth shedding tears over? Or is there another reason that defies logic?" The orangutan fired a barrage of difficult-to-answer questions at me.

"I was reviewing what was and wasn't accomplished during our daily work evaluation. However, what often disappoints me is the inequality in our collaboration. Our decades of conservation experience have shown that this work requires teamwork and joint effort. Hence, personal feelings should take a back seat, and the ego that says, 'This is my job, not ours,' must be set aside. Only then can our teamwork become stronger."

"My friend, in life, sadness, anxiety, bitterness, and disappointment can happen to anyone and at any time, and sometimes, one after the other. Just like rain and shine, only God, the owner of Life, knows with certainty. However, when your desires or expectations are not fulfilled or met, your feelings can get hurt and lead to feeling let down," he added.

"True, but I just don't get it. When we were discussing activities, for example, why are some of my colleagues overly sensitive and easily offended, while others are quick to anger? Then there are those who talk about spending like money is no object but refuse to help raise funds. Don't they realize that we also have the right to be annoyed, even angry? I've chosen to stay quiet and reflect on finding solutions to the problem, but at times, I can't hold back my frustration. And then, as you saw earlier, I seethed silently, and tears spilled from my eyes," I said in a flat, impassive voice.

"There are no rules that prohibit men from crying, my friend. Unfortunately, sadness is our best teacher, for a man can see further through tears than through a telescope," my companion replied with Buddha-like empathy. "Crying is how your eyes speak when your mouth is silenced, unable to explain how let down your heart feels. So, it is okay for you to escape from reality, as long as you know the way back. Go with childlike innocence, as it were, but return with maturity."

I was left speechless by the orangutan's response. Was I right to be angry? Was I justified in feeling disappointed? Or, in reality, did my year-end self-reflection show me that I was the cause of all my discontent? Could I have been my own worst enemy? The chaotic clash of wind, rain, and thunder mirrored the turmoil between my mind and my heart. I hoped that the thunder would crush my woes, along with everyone's ego, and that the rainwater would wash them all away to the estuary of peace.

"You can't start the next chapter in your life if you keep re-reading the previous pages, you know," he continued.

"But why don't my colleagues in conservation subscribe to the notion of 'united we stand'? Surely, collaborating without being easily offended, without feeling superior, or needing to control decisions would make our challenging job easier. After all, raising funds isn't easy, and thinking outside the box is required to mobilize the entire nation to participate in conservation," I continued, still trying to justify my thoughts.

"Conservation work can only be accomplished through teamwork, and that is a proven fact," the orangutan commented. "Regardless of the challenges, together you will always be stronger, even though there are times when you may be unaware that you are placing expectations on those you cannot rely on. Therefore, put your hope in God, not in men. Didn't the Scriptures contain many stories of God breaking the hearts of His beloved servants, leaving them with no more expectations of the world?"

"Ugh, why do you have to be preachy, anyway?" I said, exasperated. All I wanted was to be heard. Instead, my companion spoke of God.

You did the right thing by

"You're a Batak, right? From North Sumatra?" he asked, deflecting my complaint. "What you did—keeping to yourself, doing self-evaluation, and not letting everyone see your unhappiness—is right. Isn't there a saying in your culture that goes, '*Tangis di habunian, mengkel di na patar?*' Doesn't it mean that if your hurt and disappointments are expressed through tears, they should be hidden behind a smile? Therefore, refrain from showing your problems to the world. Instead, present people with a smile so that everyone can move forward optimistically. Those who are strong-hearted are not necessarily the ones who never cry; rather, they are the ones who remain steadfast in their commitment, even when they experience hurt from many others."

"So, shedding tears of disappointment because your feelings are hurt as a result of working together in orangutan conservation is not forbidden, right?" I replied with a wry smile, feeling vindicated by what the orangutan had just told me.

"No, it is not. But when you experience a letdown, accept it with an open heart. Not everything in life has to be obtained or go according to plan. You can plan, but the final decision is in the hands of God, the owner of Life." Again, my companion shared his words of wisdom. Then he continued, "If there were no storms, the rainbows would not appear. Therefore, learn from the storms that befall you, since rainbows only form after the rain. Likewise, fortitude only develops once pain cuts deep into the heart. And remember, my friend, disappointment is simply God's way of saying, 'I have something better for you.'"

Unbeknownst to me, the downpour had subsided, and the thunderstorm had waned in its ferocity. Although it was still drizzling, I could faintly hear the voice of my friend, the orangutan, quoting a tongue-in-cheek Indonesian saying: *"Bekerjalah sepenuh hati dan bukan sepenuh jiwa, palingan kamu sakit hati dan bukan sakit jiwa"* (loosely translated as "Work with your whole heart, not with your whole soul; at the very least, you'll end up with a broken heart rather than a 'broken mind', i.e., go crazy").

"Therefore, maintain your emotional and mental sanity. We orangutans need you to stay healthy, both in mind and body. Remember, being healthy is more than just caring about what you eat. It's also about taking care of your thoughts and feelings. Nothing in this world can torture you more than your own mind," he admonished gently.

⁓ ∂ɣ∂ ⁓

That day, I learned important lessons from my orangutan friend. The <u>first</u> was the importance of working with an open heart, but not so open that you get emotionally hurt or, worse, end up with a "broken mind"—going crazy. The <u>second</u> was to maintain the spirit of cooperation in conservation, even though, along the way, not everything can go according to plan.

Although reality doesn't always match our expectations, it doesn't mean we should be discouraged. Let's use the piano keys as an analogy: the white keys represent happiness, and the black keys, sadness. When we play the piano, we will inevitably realize that the black keys also play an important role in creating the music we hear.

Therefore, understanding is the key to overcoming disappointment because, behind every wound, there is always a beautiful story waiting to be told. As my orangutan companion reminded me, "Forget the bitterness, but never forget the lessons. Disappointments and hurt feelings have no place in a heart full of gratitude."

Thank you for teaching me these lessons, my friend.

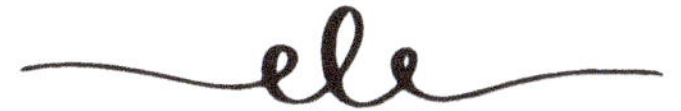

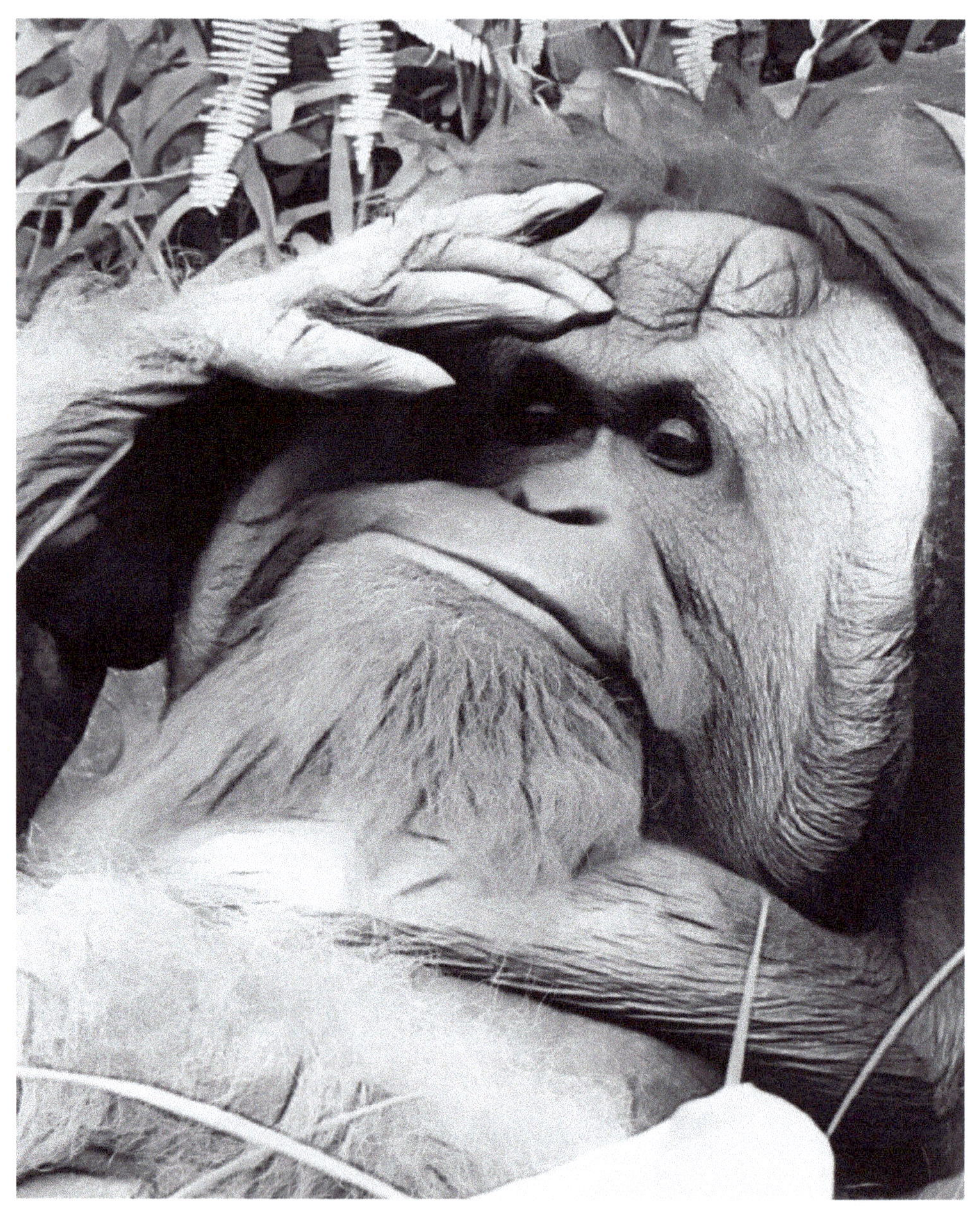

"Quam bene vivas refert, non quam diu'
—what matters is how well you live, not how long"
- Lucius Annaeus Seneca, Stoic Roman philosopher

Chapter 22

Orangutan Deserves Freedom, Too

All of God's creatures share one similarity: the desire to live freely and independently in their promised land with Him, the Creator. Many nations have fought, with millions of lives sacrificed, to achieve what is known as independence—that is, freedom from colonialism. Yet, according to the French philosopher Albert Camus, freedom should bring about change for the better.

My thoughts turned to my friend Suja, an orangutan who now roams freely in the release forest of Bukit Baka-Bukit Raya National Park in Central Kalimantan. Suja was once a victim of illegal wildlife trafficking before she was repatriated from Thailand. She must have been overjoyed to regain her freedom. As I thought about her, our minds seemed to connect, and we ended up having an engrossing, albeit imaginary, conversation.

"Hello, my friend, why do you appear to be so pensive? Isn't today the day you celebrate your country's independence from colonialism, and thus your freedom?" Suja said, her greeting diverting me from my thoughts.

"Hmm, I've been pondering the independence we've had for decades. In many ways, it seems like not everyone has freedom. It troubles me that some still lack independence. From your greeting, it sounds as if you're not part of this independent nation. Why don't you feel free now that this country has gained its independence? Don't you live in Indonesia, too?" I asked her.

"Hahaha... There is no doubt that Indonesia is independent. But have you, the people of Indonesia, ever considered that we orangutans enjoyed greater freedom during the colonial era? Have you ever thought about how this country's freedom has allowed liberated humans in the nation to treat us orangutans any way they want?"

"Wow, that's quite the criticism, isn't it?" I said to her, a little taken aback by her reply.

"So, let me ask you this," Suja inquired. "What exactly does independence mean to you, or to those of you working in conservation? Even after decades of independence, the people of Indonesia are still seen as incapable of conservation. Your TV programs prefer to feature Westerners doing conservation work rather than Indonesians.

To us, independence should be 'responsible freedom'— the freedom to take conscientious actions that do not infringe on the freedom of others. Similarly, we want your work to be better and done in a good way. A good goal can't be considered good if it is implemented recklessly, without adhering to rules, or by justifying any means to achieve it.

Work should be done ethically and properly. So, manage your emotions and every step of your work carefully," she said, explaining her thoughts.

"That's certainly true, Suja," I replied. "But the media tends to approach everything, including conservation-related matters, from a business perspective because they want to make a profit. Therefore, they seek to raise awareness through comparison—'Even foreigners care about conservation, why don't our own people care?'"

"Well, that's just it," she responded. "Did the freedom fighters who fought for independence back then have business in mind? No, they didn't. Whether they realized it or not, they agreed with the opinion of Jean-Paul Sartre, a French philosopher, who said that the basic predicament of humanity is freedom itself. In his legendary lecture on existentialism, Sartre declared, 'Man is condemned to be free,' implying that man is not born with a predetermined purpose or nature. In other words, humans are free to choose their own course in life without any external influence. Therefore, with that freedom, humans can choose to act, even though, in doing so, they sometimes suppress the freedom of others," she said.

Realizing the truth in what Suja said, I quietly responded, "But it is often necessary to remain silent first, to reflect before taking action," still trying to justify my understanding of Sartre's idea.

"That's smart, but more often, people's deliberation prior to taking action is motivated by economic interests. Do you remember how the Buddha, Siddhartha Gautama, sought wisdom by withdrawing from society and living an ascetic life under the Bodhi Tree in the Uruvela Forest for six years until he attained enlightenment?" she asked. "Wisdom is the ultimate goal to be achieved."

"On this Independence Day, humanity must strive to understand its role as rational beings and view events from a positive and logical perspective. Do not stand by and allow the actions of others to cause emotional wounds. Do not let bitter experiences shackle you. Your work in conservation is not always pleasant, and at times, it can be emotionally painful, right? Regardless of how bitter and painful the Buddha's asceticism was, he ultimately found that the bitterness led to perfect wisdom. You've probably experienced that too," Suja explained clearly.

"But we're not Siddhartha," I countered, disagreeing with what she said, despite knowing it was true.

"Hahaha... So, learn from the experience of others, including from us orangutans. Didn't Seneca say, 'Quam bene vivas refert, non quam diu'—'what matters is how well you live, not how long'? Let me tell you about Seneca before you ask who he is. Lucius Annaeus Seneca was a Stoic Roman philosopher during the Silver Age of Latin literature. He was also known as the tutor to Emperor Nero, even though his life ended at Nero's hands," Suja explained, adding tidbits of information.

"That's interesting. I'll look up more about who Seneca is later," I said, a little embarrassed. Of course, I knew of Seneca. He was one of the philosophers whose name often came up in Philosophy of Science discussions when I was in college, but now I've forgotten his theories and thoughts, while Suja could explain Seneca's ideas easily.

"Okay," she said. "Thank you for returning us home to the forest. This is our promised land with the Creator. You have set us free to be independent in our habitat because of your love for us. Love is the only freedom in this world because it liberates. No force of nature, nor any human effort, can alter the course of love. As Seneca said, 'The world is sleeping, and people are dreaming. But tomorrow, when dawn comes, we can make our dreams come true.' My friend, you and your peers working in orangutan conservation have made our dreams of being free in nature a reality. As a result, we have been returned to the forest, our true home," Suja said gratefully.

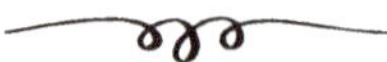

As I pondered my conversation with my orangutan friend in the release forest, I tried to digest what she had said about the meaning of freedom in simple terms. The essence of it was responsible freedom. Although I didn't regret what I had done during this time of independence, the discussion made me realize the regrets I still carried because the many things I wished I had done to make this freedom more meaningful for all of His creation..

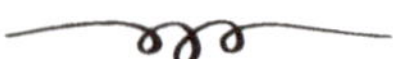

As we Indonesians joyously exclaim 'Merdeka!' (meaning freedom) to commemorate our Independence Day, we must also remember the other creatures living on this land we call Indonesia. They, too, should be part of this independent nation. To make that possible, we can liberate wildlife, such as orangutans, and give them the freedom to live in the forest, not in cages.

Let's not confine wildlife to cages in the name of love and caregiving. That is pure selfishness, not love. Wildlife belongs in nature. This is a fundamental truth, just as love liberates. We have our independence so that we can free others—our fellow beings, such as orangutans and other wildlife, who are also God's creations.

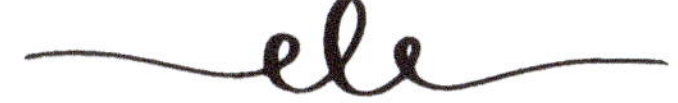

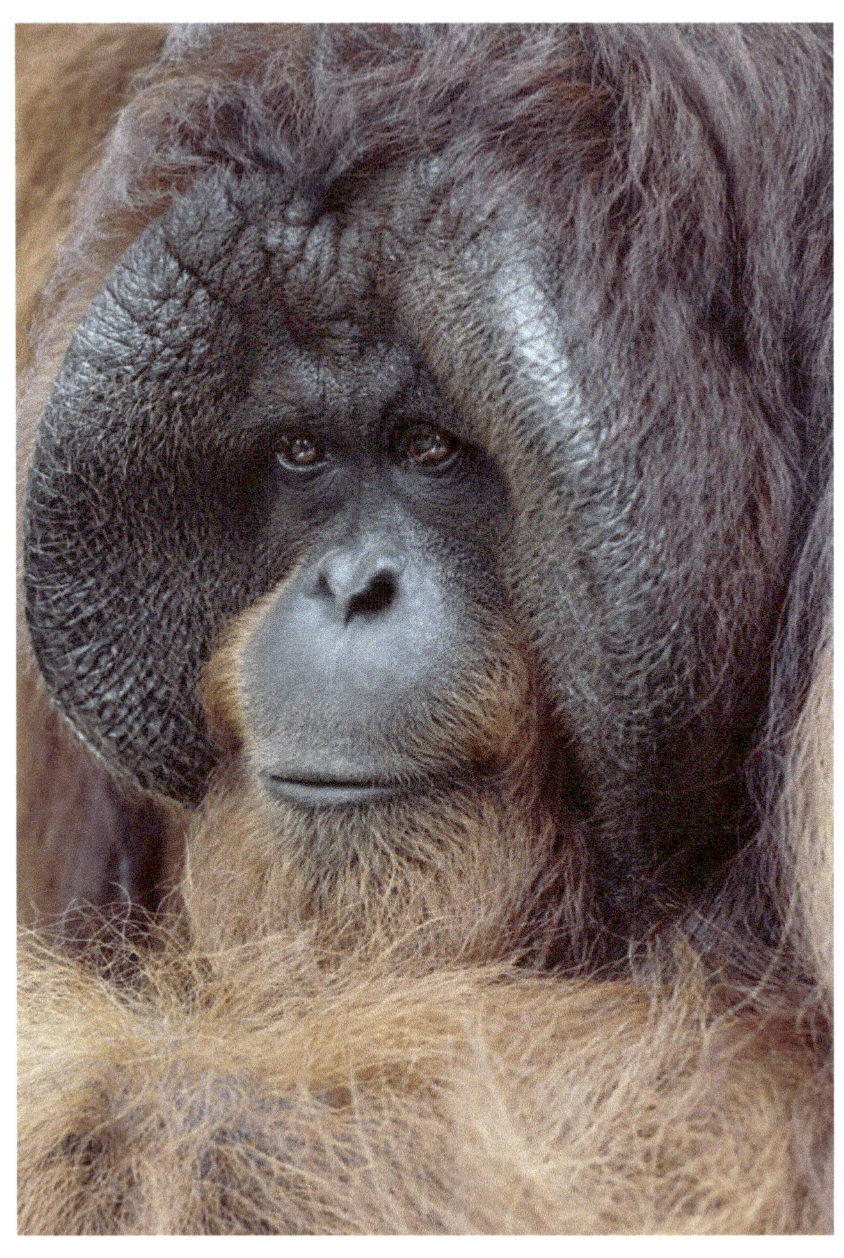

"Better late than never"

Chapter 23

Is Romeo Truly Free?

Afternoons after the rain are the most enjoyable time for me to take a walk around the Samboja Lestari Orangutan Rehabilitation Centre in East Kalimantan. The damp earth and the smell of leaf litter on the forest floor add to the romantic atmosphere of the forest. I find that enjoying the sunset while photographing orangutans is a luxury in itself.

That day, with my camera in hand, I made my way toward the man-made islands. I stopped in front of one of the islands, nestled among the others. It was inhabited by Romeo, a 30-year-old male orangutan. I spent some time trying to capture him with my camera. At different times I had to shift to the right and left, move forward, and even crouch down to get the right angle for a good shot.

An hour later, I felt satisfied with the pictures I'd taken. I spent the rest of the afternoon sitting on a wooden bench, observing Romeo's behavior. He was aware that he was being watched. He shifted his large body to hide in the bushes as much as possible, but he kept his eyes on me. I am not sure how many orangutans this has happened with, but once our eyes connected, we greeted each other and eventually had a conversation through our eyes.

"Hello, my friend. You love the atmosphere at Samboja Lestari after the rain, don't you?" greeted Romeo from the thick bushes on the man-made island at Samboja.

"Yes, I really enjoy it. It truly is a lovely afternoon," I warmly replied.

"It is indeed a beautiful afternoon. However, I couldn't help but notice that your mind seems to be wandering elsewhere, even though you are only a few meters away from me. If you don't mind my asking, what are you thinking about?" He seemed to be able to read my mind.

"Oh, it's nothing serious. It's just that my mind can't stop thinking about what people said when we moved you from the enclosure to the man-made island," I explained, sharing the thoughts in my mind.

"Hahaha... you don't need to dwell on all comments, especially if they stress you out. We orangutans need you to have fresh ideas and a positive attitude, not to be anxious due to other people's judgments. Just think—some of my friends and I would never have been able to leave our cages and experience nature if you were only fixated on people's opinions. Ever heard of the Latin phrase: 'Si quid audis, alii ridebunt te?' It means if you listen to everyone, others will laugh at you. So, come on, cheer up and just do your job as best you can."

"Here's the thing," I said to him. "Someone asked me what the difference is for you between living in a cage and being on a man-made island that's not even that big—only 4,000 square meters, less than a hectare. To them, it's all the same. So, what accomplishment is there for us to be proud of?"

"Woah, take it easy. You work in conservation, so you shouldn't expect popularity or to be recognized as someone great. Conservation work is like walking a silent path. Now, as for where we live, whether being in a cage or on a man-made island, it's the same for us, too. It's true what the person said—neither is a natural forest. But why don't you ask us orangutans, especially me, Romeo, what we think about it? Let me tell you a story, but listen closely and don't drift off into a daydream. Your mind must be here with me and my tale."

"Alright. I'm ready to listen to what you're about to tell me," I said.

"I, Romeo, am a 30-year-old male orangutan who represents the many orangutans who have lived in cages for many years. I was repatriated to Indonesia when I was six years old and brought directly to the Orangutan Rehabilitation Centre Foundation, which, at that time, was still located at Wanariset, a tropical forest research station owned by the Forestry Research and Development Agency of the Ministry of Forestry of Indonesia in East Kalimantan. A few years later, I was transferred to the Samboja Lestari Orangutan Rehabilitation Center in East Kalimantan.

I have a dark and sad past. I used to live in a zoo in Taiwan, where I was confined to a small cage and displayed as an animal exhibit. I still clearly remember how, back then, I couldn't move freely or do anything without being watched by people. But then, my fate changed in an instant. I was repatriated and brought back to Indonesia. At Samboja Lestari, my hopes were reignited when I entered the rehabilitation program. However, bitter reality once again blocked my path to freedom in the wild.

When I arrived in 1993, my test results showed that I was positive for Hepatitis B, a viral disease that is easily transmitted between orangutans and humans. The medical team immediately separated the Hepatitis B-positive orangutans from the healthy ones to prevent transmission within the orangutan population. For me and many other orangutans there, it felt like a nightmare. It meant we had to return to our cages and could not join the Forest School program. Our hope of being free in the forest was shattered.

It took two decades for medical science to confirm that Hepatitis B in orangutans (Orangutan hepadnavirus) occurs naturally in the wild and is harmless. In fact, according to research, the virus has long evolved with orangutans, helping to build our natural immune system without posing a threat to our survival," he explained.

"That's right. The findings from this orangutan Hepatitis B research were good news for both you and us! It meant that you and your friends, who had the same condition, could still socialize with other orangutans and even be released. But after 30 years of living in a confined space, we were concerned whether you and your similarly afflicted friends could develop the skills needed to survive in the wild," I said slowly, expressing how unprepared we had been to release him into the forest.

"Freedom is the birthright of all beings, without exception, but that fact is often overlooked," he said. "But for me and the other orangutans in the same predicament, freedom was something we hadn't known in years. The #OrangutanFreedom# campaign had reached our ears, and we continued to dream that one day, the right to be free from our cages would come our way."

"Yes, we tried our best to make your dream a reality because it was our dream, too." My throat tightened with emotion, and I could barely utter a word in response after hearing the words Romeo spoke from the bottom of his heart. I couldn't help but wonder what it would have been like if I had endured what he had gone through for as long as he had. It had been a long wait—a very long wait.

"Hey, you. Don't get lost in your thoughts. I haven't finished my story yet. Save your contemplation for later, during your bedtime musings in the camp," he reminded me, signaling that he wanted to continue the conversation.

"Oh... sorry, Romeo. Alright, I'm ready to hear the rest of it."

"Have you ever read the words of Heraclitus, an ancient Greek philosopher? He once wrote, 'You cannot step into the same river twice, for other waters are continually flowing on.' This means that, although the location may be the same, time and events can never return.

So, even though the orangutan rehabilitation center has a Forest School program and pre-release islands to prepare orangutans with the skills they need to survive in the wild, I once thought that I, Romeo, had missed out on that opportunity. I thought I could not learn in Forest School with the younger, more agile orangutans," Romeo thoughtfully explained.

"Hang on, Romeo, but we didn't give up," I exclaimed. "Because we still wanted you to be free, our first step was to move you to a pre-release island so you could learn the basic skills necessary by observing your peers in an open, outdoor environment."

"The man-made islands are specifically designed to train orangutans to live independently after completing all stages of Forest School. They allow you to live in the open and learn to socialize with other individuals, just like in the wild. As Tito Livio, a Roman historian (living between 64-59 BC), once said: 'Potius sero quam nunquam,' meaning, 'Better late than never,'" I told him.

Romeo looked intently into my eyes before continuing his response. "I am very grateful for your efforts in placing me on the man-made island. This is the first time in my 24 years of life here that I have been able to experience the outside world, without the bars of a cage.

Being able to see the stars, the moon, the rain, the sun, and the night sky makes this freedom even more meaningful. Believe me, my friend, for us orangutans who have been trapped in cages for far too long, experiencing nature as I am now brings us great peace. By moving us from our cages to these man-made islands, I am reminded of what Albert Camus, a French philosopher, once said: 'Freedom is nothing but a change for the better,'" Romeo said sincerely.

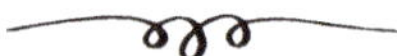

My conversation with Romeo at that time was enlightening. I listened to every word he said, observed his body language, and watched the expression in his eyes—yes, his eyes shone with clarity, alive and sparkling.

It is certainly true what Khalil Gibran once wrote: "Life without liberty is like a body without spirit." I had proof of it in Romeo. His life's journey, the pains and sorrows that colored it until the day he was moved from his enclosure to a man-made island, and the changes he experienced after he felt free, must be understood through his eyes—the eyes of an orangutan.

That's why, in all circumstances, remember: "Try first, then tell. Understand first, then answer. Think first, then speak. Listen first, then give judgment. Work first, then hope," said Socrates, the Greek philosopher, eloquently.

Thank you, and God bless you, Romeo!

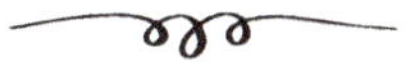

In Loving Memory of Romeo

This chapter is dedicated to Romeo, who passed away on July 31, 2024, at the age of 38.

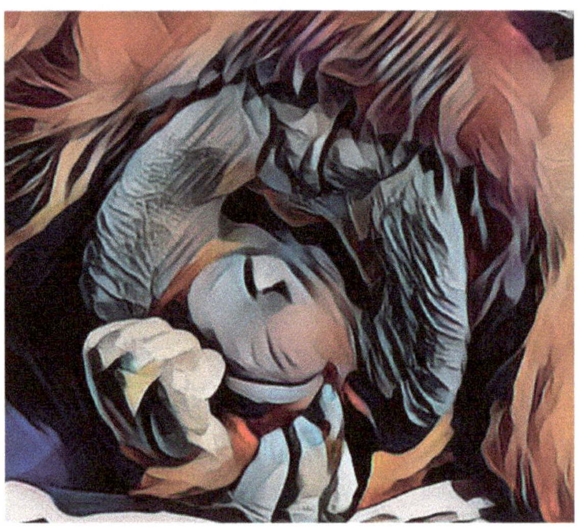

After 25 years of being confined to a cage due to health issues, Romeo was moved to an island sanctuary at Samboja Lestari in 2017. As mentioned in this story, he lacked the necessary survival skills to return to the wild, but we are grateful that he was able to spend the final years of his life roaming freely on a lush island, with sunlight on his face and no bars obstructing his view.

Freedom is indeed a fundamental right for all living beings. Happy trails, Romeo. Thank you for the lessons you've taught us!

Enjoy your freedom!

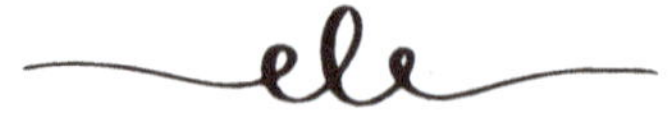

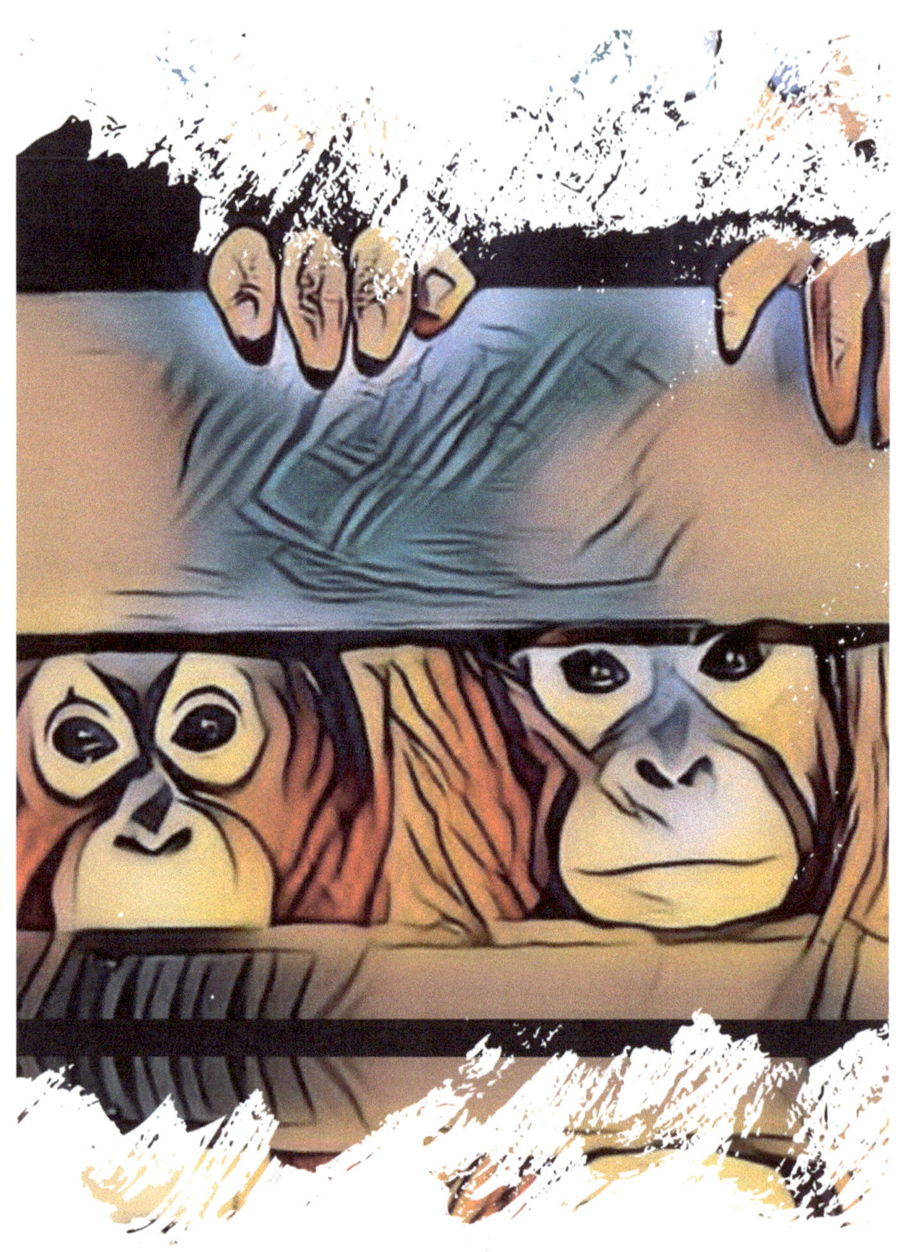

I hear the chatter of Judas' children,
Louder than the chainsaw's hum,
They busy themselves with schemes,
Worshiping the wealth of their dreams,
All the while stealing wives,
and even our brothers' heaven.

Remind them of the night's dark tale,
In the Garden of Gethsemane,
Was it Him, or was it they,
Who bore the ultimate sorrow?

- RWW -

Chapter 24

Don't Give Us a Judas Kiss

Mardalan au marsada sada
(I am walking alone)

Laos di langlang i do au tarlungun lungun
(In the silence I embrace my longing)

Manetek iluki da inang da sian mata
(My tears are falling)

Marningot lakka ki dainang laos so marujung
(Why are my steps still halting)

The rain was still soaking the earth. A steaming cup of coffee accompanied me as I worked from home. *"Mardalan Ahu"*, a track from my laptop's playlist, began to play as I opened my archives and browsed old images of orangutans. I spotted the one that had won a photo competition. I let out a heavy sigh.

The expression in the young orangutan's eyes in that picture truly pierced my heart. I felt deeply heartbroken. I slowly drifted into a long reverie, not about the competition journey—

from submitting the photo to winning and earning the title of champion—but about these young orangutans and the story behind the picture. Soon, I found myself drifting even deeper, until I was drawn into an imaginary conversation with Taymur, one of the orangutans in the photo—a juvenile we had repatriated from Kuwait.

"How are you, my friend?" I greeted Taymur, who was sitting quietly in the corner of his cage. "You must be happy to be back in Indonesia and to be rehabilitated so you can return to the forest."

"Yes, of course, I'm happy, but I'm also sad at the same time," he said, almost impassively.

"Oh? Why are you sad?"

"Have you forgotten? I am one of the many victims of the illegal orangutan trade, sold overseas by unscrupulous people. Thanks to orangutan warriors like you, we were able to return to Indonesia. However, we orangutan children should never have had to go through this ordeal. Think about it! Those people took us away from the forest, and then, under the guise of their love for wildlife, some kept us in cages in their yards. Do you consider that an act of kindness? Is that the solution? Is there any conservation effort there? Why aren't they helping to restore and protect our forests? Instead of loving and protecting us, they are taking us away from our natural habitat. It's so stupid and utterly ridiculous!"

I fell silent when I heard his indignant speech. "Yes, I know," I said, though it was more out of my desire to empathize than from any true understanding.

"I believe you *do* know that very well, my friend, including the reasoning behind why God placed us in the forest. Never mind turning away from what God has destined for us; it never even occurred to us to be corrupt. But alas, some of your kind not only took us and sold us, but they even killed our mothers! Do you realize that without our mothers' deaths, they never could have taken us and sold us on the black market? Never!" His voice hardened, and anger was etched on his face.

"Yes, you're right."

"Now let me ask you another question. Why were we put up for sale? Was it for our benefit—in our best interest? Not at all. We were sold out of arrogance and ignorance! This applies to the sellers, the buyers, and anyone else acting as an accomplice to the perpetrators in the vast network of illegal trade. We haven't even begun to address the deforestation that is slowly depleting the forests. And all of this was done by your people, not mine! What benefit have we gained from this? Absolutely none, my friend. Then, ironically, they bought us in the name of caring for wildlife, citing our status as an endangered species. The most despicable part was that they set an incredibly high price for us!"

"I condemn that, as well."

"We should not have to endure this, my friend. Did any of them think about restoring the forest and taking care of it? Hardly any. Ironic, truly ironic! Even though only 3% of our DNA is supposedly different from humans', it is implied that you are superior to us. But, the behaviors of these people show the opposite. You know, although we are considered lesser than you, we are still grateful to God for being born as orangutans. Meanwhile, your people continue to nurture their delusion of superiority. What a shallow understanding!"

Taymur paused for a moment before continuing his reproach. 'If only people would use their brains, even just a little, they would realize that the idea of buying us and keeping us in captivity is not the same as saving us in the long run. Instead, it only fuels rampant poaching, which undermines conservation efforts. It's like the problem of having 1% of people continue using air rifles, even when 99% have stopped. This makes the effort to ensure everyone's total safety pointless."

"So, please remember this, my friend," he said, looking at me pointedly. "Don't let people imprison us behind their houses in the name of caring for and protecting wild animals, even when they proudly proclaim that what they are doing is a rescue effort. Because this is no different than Judas' kiss to Jesus in the Garden of Gethsemane! In fact, in our prayer to God, we once said, 'O God, please save us from those who claim to be making conservation efforts, when, in reality, they are taking us away from the purpose for which You created us.'"

I was so stunned that I couldn't speak. His words shook me to my core, plunging me into a state of despair.

My imaginary conversation with Taymur, the young orangutan, reminded me of what Descartes, the father of modern philosophy, once said: 'Cogito, Ergo Sum' (I think, therefore I am). In the name of our love for wildlife, we sometimes unknowingly treat these animals based on our egoistic desires, rather than respecting their *fitrah*—their inherent nature, the way they were meant to be in the wild.

His words about Judas's kiss jolted me. My mind immediately flew to the story of Jesus' crucifixion, which began in the Garden of Gethsemane, when Judas approached and kissed Jesus as though he loved Him, when in reality, the opposite was true. As I looked into the eyes of the young orangutan we repatriated from overseas, I couldn't help but think that there was no weapon more cruel and deadly than Judas's Kiss, for I have seen the evidence of humans' 'false love' betraying their true nature. Indeed, I admit that Taymur was right—that he and the other orangutan children should have been in their mothers' arms in the forest. Period.

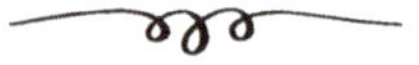

My friends, in our orangutan conservation efforts, we need support from many parties so that these orangutans can return to their homes in the forest. Please do not give us the 'Judas's Kiss,' because the truth is, such betrayal will only bring disaster to those who commit it. Understand that keeping wild animals (especially orangutans) as pets is no different than the false love depicted in Judas's Kiss.

"No weapon is half as deadly as 'Judas's Kiss'. We at BOSF need your support to return more orangutans to their home, the forest—but please, do not offer us a Judas kiss."

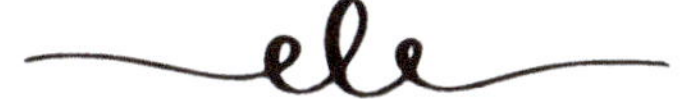

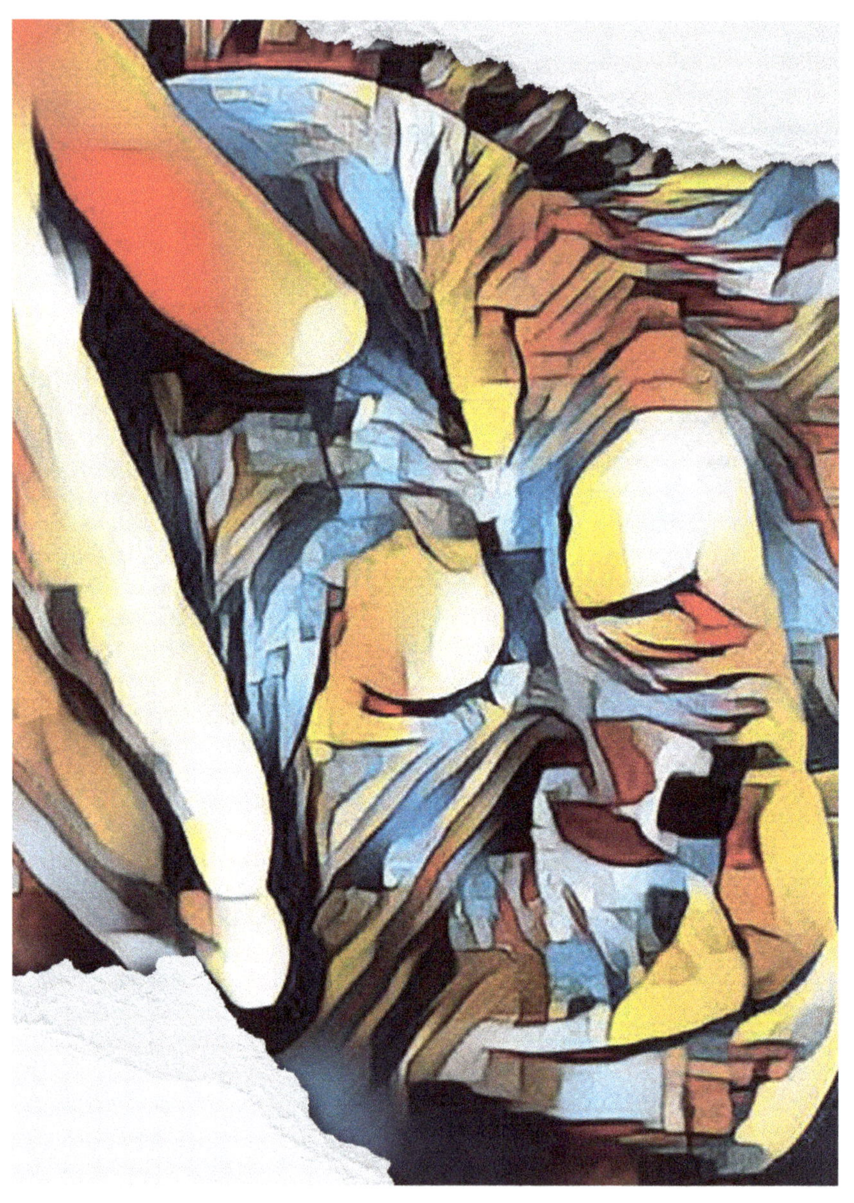

When the river speaks,
Have we listened to its soft voice?
When the river ceases,
Will we remember its wise words?

Chapter 25

Reflection from the River

The Post Release Monitoring (PRM) activities conducted after the release of orangutans into the forest are both exciting and exhausting. In addition to directly tracking the orangutans' movements and progress in the wild, we must also observe, record, and document their behavior while ensuring they are capable of surviving in their natural habitat. These precautions are especially important given the lengthy re-education process these previously domesticated orangutans underwent to prepare them for reintroduction to the wild.

In the forest, orangutans are incredibly nimble, able to move horizontally through the canopy, swinging from one tree to another. However, the same cannot be said for the monitoring team. The team must climb up and down cliffs—depending on the terrain—often sweating profusely. In fact, it is not uncommon for them to slip and get injured. So, it is not an exaggeration to describe the PRM team as those who work with blood and sweat, not just sweat and tears.

One time, I joined a PRM group to monitor an orangutan. We woke up very early, at 3 o'clock in the morning, and just an hour later, we set off for the orangutan's nesting site. Our first task was to ensure we were already stationed under the orangutan's nest long before he woke up. We spent the rest of the day recording the orangutan's behavior, including his feeding patterns. The monitoring itself began when the orangutan woke up and continued until the afternoon, when he prepared a new nest to serve as his sleeping platform.

For us, the monitoring team, the only time to relax between tasks is usually during lunchtime. Imagine having lunch on the bank of a small river with its crystalline water— it's such a luxury! The packed lunch we bring from our camp in the forest, combined with the view of the pristine river, replenishes our depleted energy.

So, when lunchtime arrived, I took the time to truly savor my meal while soaking in the atmosphere of the clear, calm river. We could see ourselves mirrored in the water, and the reflection staring back at us was almost flawless. Then, flashbacks of events surfaced in my mind, one after another, including memories from years ago when we surveyed release sites. These surveys are both obligatory and necessary. The locations chosen for release are typically remote and isolated, with the hope that the released orangutans will be able to adapt to their new environment with minimal to no disturbance or disruption.

As I reflected on these surveys, I was reminded of a time when we inspected a forest I had visited and stayed in for quite a while. The forest had previously been a timber concession (HPH, in Indonesian). It was quite a coincidence. Images of the dense woods and the access road, from the time it was still a concession, remained vividly imprinted in my mind. Later, a stream of memories from other forests and previous releases alternated in my mind, including the faces of the orangutans we had already released.

"Hello, my friend. You look contemplative. What are you thinking about?"

I heard the voice in my mind, but when I looked around, there was no one there.

"Hey!" The voice returned, and I noticed Hamzah, my orangutan friend whom we had previously released in a restoration forest, perched on a tree branch directly above my head. Our eyes met through the reflection on the surface of the water. There was nothing shameful or self-conscious about it, because even the heavens deign to reflect in the lowly puddle.

I realized I must have heard the voice of Hamzah, a male orangutan who had become the dominant male (alpha male) in Kehje Sewen Restoration Forest in East Kalimantan. This unique name is derived from the local Dayak Wehea language: 'Kehje' means orangutan, and 'Sewen' means forest. So, the name of the forest essentially means "Orangutan Forest."

"He must have many hot topics to discuss, considering he has been a jungle dweller for many years," I thought to myself.

"Hello, Hamzah. I'm not sure why you've suddenly appeared in my mind just now. Is it because you have a story to tell?" I asked.

"I greeted you not because I wanted to share a story, but because your silence and the reverberation of your brainwaves caught our attention amidst all the activities in the forest. So I should be the one to ask, 'What's going on with you, my friend?'" he responded with a question. And, as usual with all my imaginary conversations with the orangutans, this dialogue with Hamzah also made my brow furrow, as it evoked such deep memories.

"I remember how the release process was planned for a past release. The reflection on this clear river water brings back beautiful memories of the preparation, despite how difficult it felt at the time. It's true what the wise say: difficult and burdensome situations become sweet memories after we've gone through them, so much so that we can even make self-deprecating jokes about ourselves."

Hamzah seemed to think for a moment before commenting.

"Tell us the story, so we orangutans can also learn from what you've done. However, if possible, don't tell us how difficult it was to assess our food availability, potential threats, or habitat suitability. We'd like to hear something else," he replied with a smile.

"Oh, so you want to hear about our experiences, including the absurdities that happened, huh? Or the story of how downcast and defeated we were during the preparation and implementation of the survey?" I said evasively, reluctant to share our tales of woe and folly.

"Don't jump to negative conclusions, my friend. Don't we need courage to do introspection if we want to improve? And isn't there always a valuable lesson to be learned from every painful experience, as long as we are willing to reflect on ourselves?" he said wisely.

I was taken aback; his words struck me deeply. Just moments ago, I had seen the reflection of my weary face on the surface of the clear water. Now, Hamzah, the orangutan, was inviting me to look for insights beyond what had already transpired. I remembered that my late father once said, "Learn from people who are truly wise, not from those who merely appear wise." Maybe it was time for me to learn from orangutans.

"Alright, I'll tell you about it. For the survey, we ventured into the forest by renting a brand-new 4WD SUV, believing this rugged vehicle would be more than capable of reaching terrain rarely visited by people. In addition, the locals helped us by supplying a car nearly 20 years older than the new rental SUV. We playfully named this old car '*Si Tua Seksi*' (The Sexy Old One).

While we were passing through a long-unused road, one of the vehicles we brought from the city finally gave up.

It broke down and was unable to continue the journey. But not so with *Si Tua Seksi*. In fact, *Si Tua Seksi* even managed to tow the much newer car out of the forest. Sometimes, in nature, technological sophistication is no match for the experience gained over time.

Later in the journey, since *Si Tua Seksi* was struggling and the overflowing river was causing flooding in the area, we decided to stay overnight in the forest. The cold of the night, the wet clothes on our bodies, and our hungry stomachs became our companions as we passed the remaining hours of the day."

"So, when you spent the night in wet clothes with an empty stomach, were you able to fall asleep, or did your mind wander, filling the night with random, wild ideas? Or were you filled with frustration, instead?" Hamzah asked curiously.

As soon as he spoke, my memory flashed back. That night, we were forced to stay overnight near a small, clear river, enjoying the reflection in the water.

"Well, my mind wandered to what BOSF (Borneo Orangutan Survival Foundation) might look like in the future—or more specifically, what the future of orangutan conservation might be," I answered. "I wondered about this because, as I gazed into the mirror-like clarity of the river, the reflection that appeared was a row of cages with different orangutan faces peering out. However, if we focus ahead with pure intention, we will realize that orangutan rehabilitation can also take place within the BOSF work area in the forest. This way, we would need fewer cages. That was one of the outcomes of my contemplation while reflecting on the clear water of the river."

"Be mindful when using clear water as a mirror, for all you can see is your own reflection. When you deliberately muddy the water, the reflection becomes obscured. In other words, introspection should be for oneself; it's not meant for others," said Hamzah the orangutan, wisely.

"Thank you, Hamzah. I agree with your thoughts. When problems arise, there's no need to fuss noisily over who is at fault. Instead, it's better to deeply reflect on ourselves and correct the situation to prevent it from happening again. Your views remind me of the Indonesian proverb: 'Ugly face, split the mirror,' which means, 'Do not blame the world for your faults.' So, indeed, introspection is key to cultivating self-awareness."

"I believe regular introspection will be beneficial for those of you working in orangutan conservation. Practicing it consistently is like having a friend who will faithfully watch over every step you take. Also, don't feel guilty, let alone burden yourself with the need to please everyone, as doing so will make your journey more difficult, or worse, hinder it. So, simply flow, like the water in front of you," Hamzah said, thoughtfully.

"And we're always stronger together than we are alone. In Congo, there's a proverb that says, 'A single bracelet does not jingle.' Essentially, it means that while individual efforts are valuable, they are often insufficient to make a significant impact. This proverb reminds us of the power of unity and collaboration—that building relationships and working together are key to creating change and achieving a common goal. By truly understanding this expression, we'll better grasp why all parties must act together to ensure the future of orangutans in the forest. So remember this adage, my friend: "If you want to go fast, walk alone. If you want to go far, walk together," Hamzah said, gently bringing our conversation to a close.

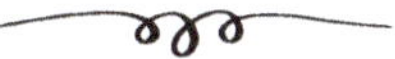

Introspection is a practice that we must incorporate into our lives. It is both an action and an awareness that we must first apply to ourselves in order to identify our true needs, so that we can make the necessary changes to become better individuals. This process of self-improvement will lead us to become more understanding and wiser in responding to both the good and bad things that happen in life. Although introspection is meant to be directed at oneself, its impact and benefits are immense for the collective.

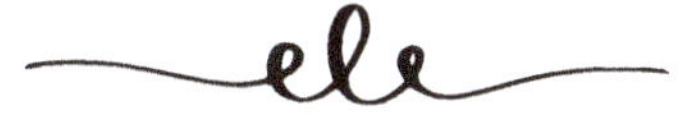

Essays & Musings

A note is a form of painting.
A painting, showing a moment of unrest,
leading to reflection on a journey,
written, hidden in silence

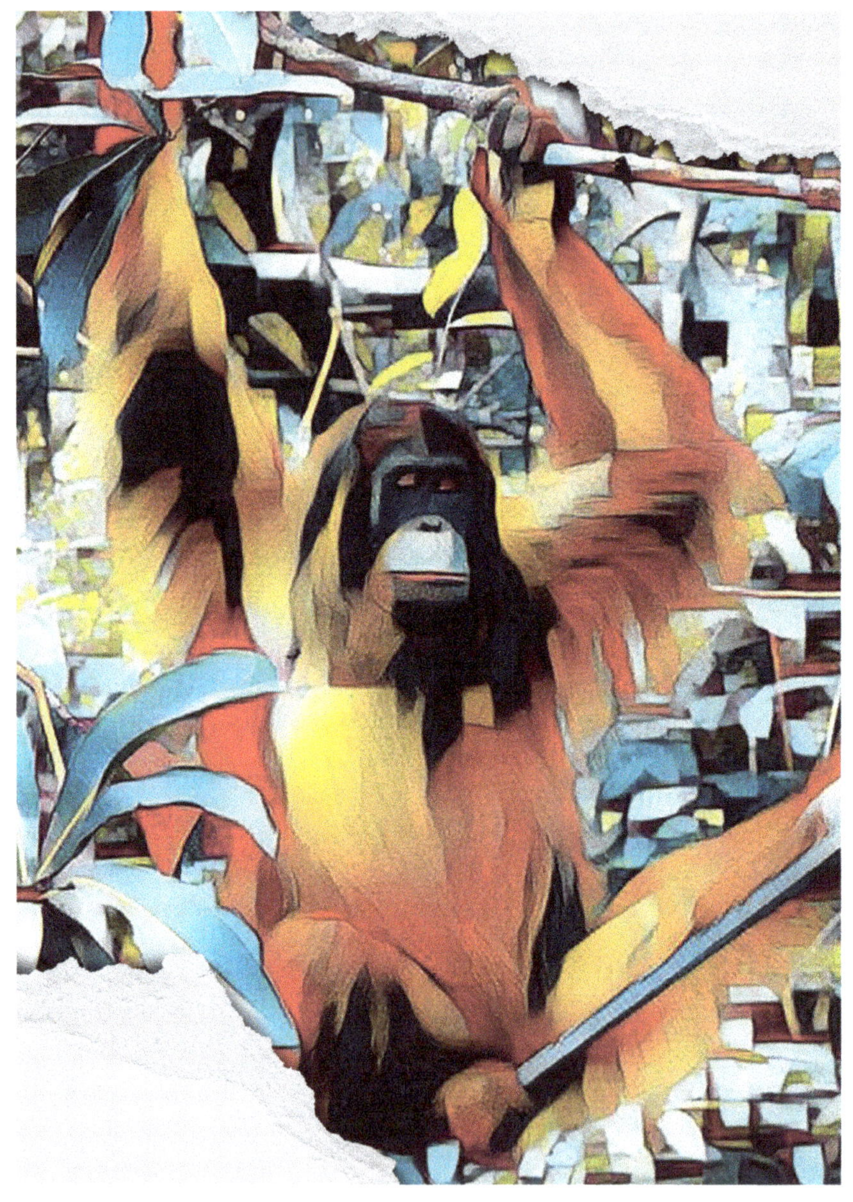

"*Spreading seeds and opening tree canopy*
so that tree seedlings can grow and thrive,
is the orangutans' ritual of worship
on this earth"

Chapter 26

A Mandate from Heaven

The Scriptures explain that God creates this world step by step, bringing it to a state of perfection and completeness. In the science of applied biology, we observe the richness of the earth's diversity, with the term 'Kingdom' used to classify all creatures and the distinctive patterns of these creatures clearly observable. I believe all of this is inseparable from the power of God, who creates the animal kingdom on this earth.

In creation, God has appointed orangutans to be forest dwellers. They have received a mandate and entrusted with the noble task of seed dispersal and caretaking of the forests, whose products and benefits are intended for all creatures on earth, including humans.

If we reflect on this, we can recognize how everything on this earth is interconnected, including the noble role carried out by orangutans. This task is a divine command, not one imposed by other creatures. If we may draw a parallel between this task and worship, the activities of spreading seeds and opening the tree canopy to allow these seeds to grow can be seen as part of the orangutans' ritual of worship on this earth. Through the results of this ritual, we humans also benefit from the forest's offerings, such as wood, and non-timber products, and the environmental services it provides, in the form of clean water and clean air.

These are all important factors in climate regulation—not only in the local environment where the animals reside, but also in how they impact the planet as a whole. Thus, orangutans play a critical role in maintaining climate stability. Consider this: through forest planting, carbon dioxide pollution can be converted into oxygen, which benefits all of us.

However, humans often make incorrect assumptions or hold biased views. When we help orangutans, we tend to believe that these rescue efforts are possible because we (humans) are in a better, superior position compared to them, solely because we see ourselves as the rulers of this earth. It is time to re-examine this distorted mindset by reflecting on how the earth is originally created in His power.

Of course, it is no coincidence that God creates this earth complete with its flora and fauna. I remember when I was in Sunday school, we were taught how God created man on the last day of creation. Let me stress the point—at the very end of creation. With this in mind, are we aware that God designed this earth so perfectly, as a manifestation of His love and compassion for us? He created all the helpers humanity could need, even before humans existed.

Without all the supporting systems that were first brought to earth, humans would certainly not be able to survive. This suggests that humans are actually the weakest of all creatures, not the strongest. Humans may appear far stronger than other species, but this is only because all the support enabling them to live has been prepared in advance. But, what happens next? Over time, humans claim to be the strongest, most dominant creature, and with their inflated egos, they feel entitled to everything on this planet. Humans even believe they have complete control over everything.

While sitting cross-legged on a piece of rattan mat at the corner of the orangutan release camp, I meditated on all of this.

How much time has passed since we, humans, have been stuck—trapped in this erroneous, flawed, and chaotic mindset that must be corrected before it is too late? It is imperative that humans respect all of His creations. This is absolute, and it is a way to manifest our gratitude for the human life that God has given us.

In the forest, I found God, who taught me about the integrity of creation. "Open yourself, and let God find you where He wants". Sometimes, it is in the silence of the forest—amidst the breeze, the rustling of leaves, the singing river, and even the faint sound of orangutans' voices heard from a distance—that we can truly feel God's presence, not in the noisy ceremonies of church service.

Remember, God has ordained orangutans as forest dwellers, granting them a full mandate—which they serve selflessly without even the slightest corruption—to be guardians and caretakers of the forest, ensuring the survival of all life on earth, including humans, until the end of their lives.

So, have we humans ever been granted the right and power by God to seize and mistreat orangutans and their forest homes, and to let them languish in cages?!

Amid the rustling trees outside the orangutan release camp, the faint notes of the song *"Apalah Arti Ibadahmu"* (What is the Meaning of Your Worship) accompanied my deepening contemplation.

> 1. What is the meaning of your worship to God,
> if there is no willingness to kneel and prostrate?
> What is the meaning of your worship to God,
> if there is no sincere heart and gratitude?
>
> *Reff:*
>> *True worship—make it an offering.*
>> *True worship—love your neighbour!*
>> *True worship that pleases God,*
>> *Honest and sincere, pure worship for God.*
>
> 2. Come, join in serving those who are troubled,
> so that (their) faith remains strong and steadfast.
> That is the task of ministry, also a calling,
> an offering that is pleasing to God.
>
> *Reff:*
>> *True worship—make it an offering...*

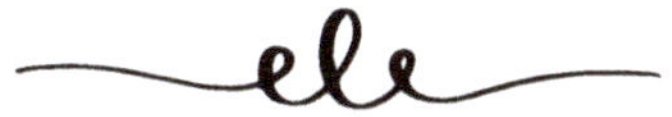

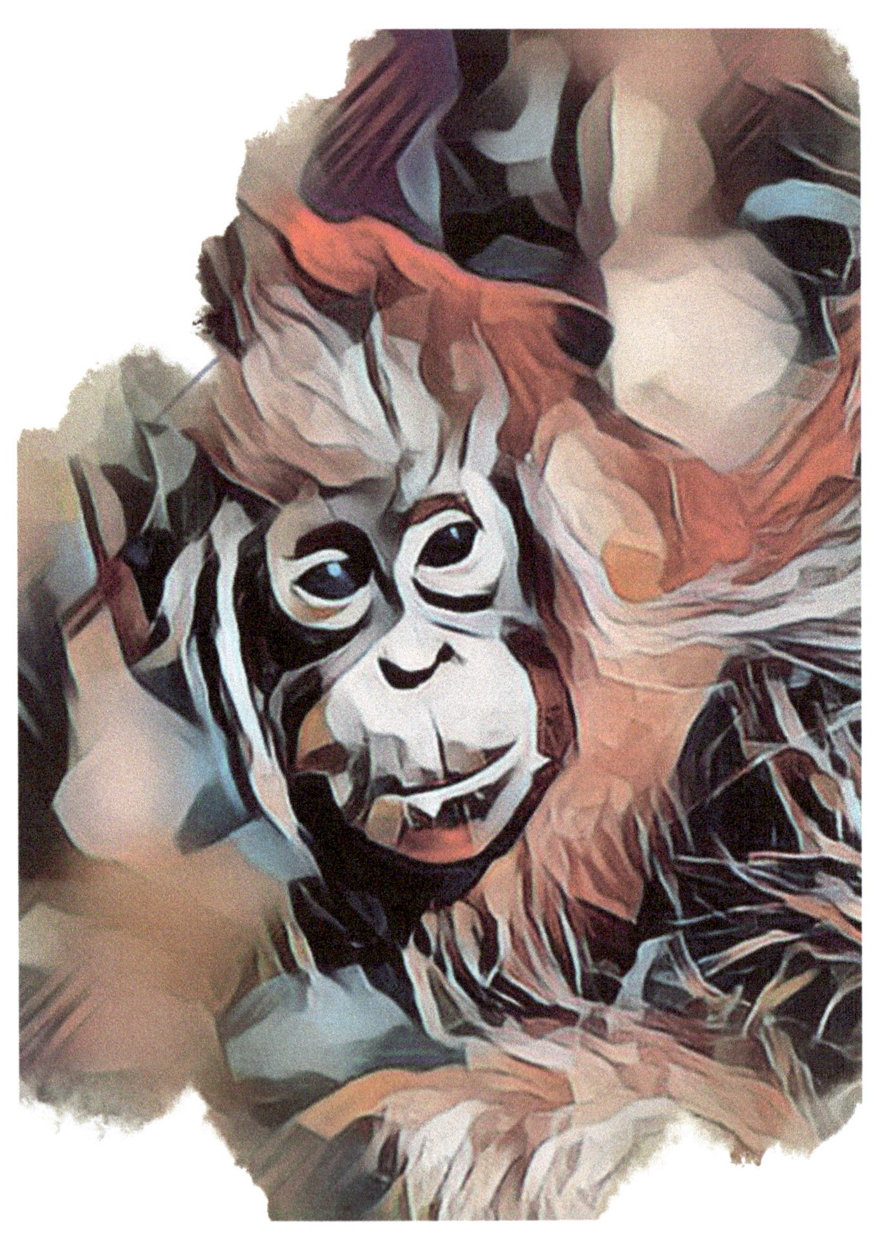

*"Helping orangutans
remain in the forest
is actually helping humankind"*

Chapter 27

A Forest to Return To

That morning, I deliberately went for a jog earlier than usual, to ensure the air I breathed was fresh before it became tainted by the pollution from the waking metropolitan city where I lived. Well, what else could we do, after all? We had to put more effort into maintaining our health, right? As usual, I chose a jogging route far from the busy main road—one lined with trees—so I could also enjoy the beautiful rays of morning sunlight filtering through the gaps in the leaves.

As I ran, listening to the melody of *'Return to Jakarta'* by the Indonesian rock legend Koes Plus, these particular lyrics transported me back to a time at the orangutan monitoring camp:

......To Jakarta I will return......

......No matter what happens......

My steps faltered, and my gaze dropped to the spot where I stood for a moment. Oh, my God. In an instant, a wave of sadness and longing washed over me. I realized that, even though I had come a long way (in my conservation work), I still had so much further to go.

I couldn't deny that I missed the forests of Kalimantan. I missed the orangutans.

Could you imagine it? If I already longed to return there, to continue the conservation work that has become a part of me, as if it were one with my soul, what about the orangutans, who yearn for their home in the forest?

Once, I asked myself: "*Why should the orangutans return to the forest?*" Then I answered, "*Of course, they should. Because there lies the heart of their lives. Because it is where they come from, where their heart lives and rejoices, where they mate and reproduce. Not to mention, it was God's own hands that brought them to this earth and placed them in the forest. Period.*"

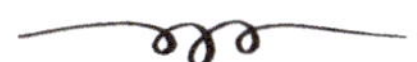

The elders said a person's soul can be seen in the look of their eyes. The eyes don't lie because they are the windows to the heart. Yes, I must admit, I got caught up in the sentimentality of orangutans the first time I saw the eyes of a baby orangutan who had lost its mother—eyes filled with sorrow, bereft after the loss of someone so precious, eyes pleading for hope, to be saved and cared for.

Hope. Let me emphasize that word to highlight its importance. Hope can be realized, but just like a seed that needs to be nurtured and cultivated, it can only be achieved through careful planning and effort. After all, isn't living without hope futile? Whether we are aware of it or not, hope is what drives us—as living beings—to grow, progress, and change for the better. Without hope, everything remains stagnant, and unmoving.

Let's return to the eyes of the orangutans. When they were babies, they were rescued from human captivity. Afterward, they went through stage after stage, learning a variety of survival skills to help them live independently in the forest, according to their God-given nature. However, in reality, after graduating from Forest School and meeting all the requirements to return to the wild, no forest is available for them to go back to. In the end, they are forced to return to cages. They have to wait for years just to reach the final stage—for the fulfillment of that final promise—to be able to return home. But for some reason, the promises made by politicians and high-ranking officials to bring the orangutans back to the forest remain difficult to fulfill.

I still remember the time I was at the corner of the orangutan monitoring camp, faintly hearing the words of an old song:

......My tears are now dry......
......To whom do I direct my hate......

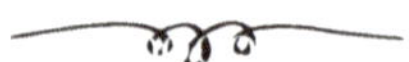

To my orangutan friends who are on the verge of extinction, please be patient. Hold on to our promise—the promise of those of us working in orangutan conservation. We will continue to strive to secure forests where you can return to the wild. We will plant the trees for you to swing and hang from, even though you cannot yet return to the forest, your true home. Rest assured, my friends, there will still be forests for you to return to. Remember that there are still many "crazy people" who are committed to planting forests. Didn't Martin Luther once say, "Even if tomorrow is the end of the world, I will still plant trees"? We are aware of our commitments and promises because if this promise is broken, even once, forgiveness means nothing.

It is not uncommon for people to consider us "crazy", because in their minds, all we do is care for orangutans. That's fine. Let them believe what they want. After all, aren't we all His creation, here on planet Earth to care for and share with one another?

Unfortunately, too many humans don't care, don't want to bother, and some still don't understand how your presence on earth is actually an extraordinary gift from God. Your presence in the forest brings it to life—contributing to clean air, clear water, and many other benefits made possible by maintaining your population on this earth. You orangutans are also an extension of God's helping hand to us humans. We, too, enjoy the fruits of your labour. Ah, if only all humans understood that helping orangutans remain in the forest is, in fact, helping humanity as well.

It's time we take care of this earth.

To my fellow humans, what will you do? Come, join us in this mission. Together, we safeguard orangutans in the forest. Together, we will build their homes. Now is the time for us to be part of the solution. It's time for us to take care of this earth. It's never too late to start a positive change—for you, for me, for all of us.

Let's unite to protect orangutans in the forest, and, together, we will build their homes. Let us be part of the solution.

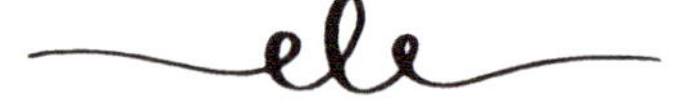

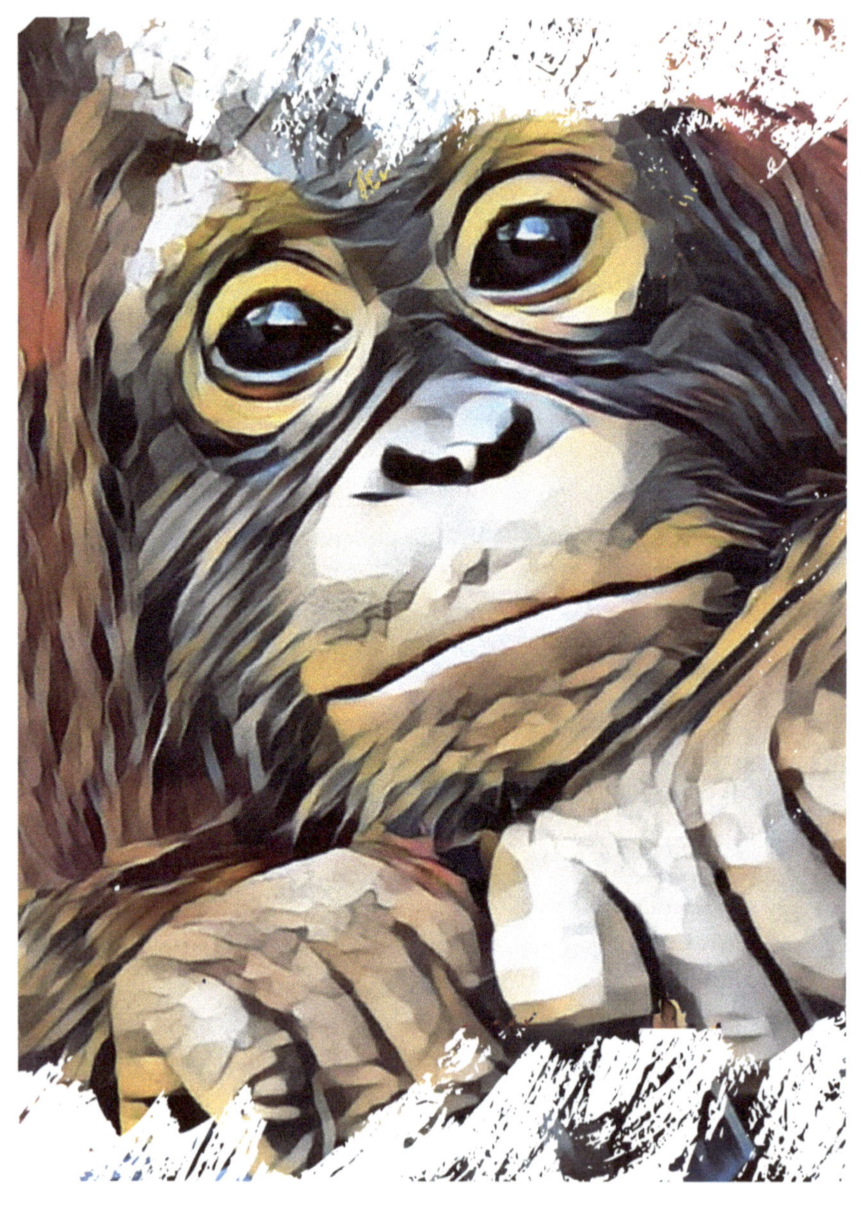

"Quo vadis?—'Where are you going?'
Let's fight for orangutans
and not abandon them!"

Chapter 28

Coronavirus Pandemic:
Quo Vadis, Rehabilitation Center?

The COVID-19 pandemic has sparked widespread media frenzy, with much of the focus on humans and the primary source of infection: wildlife, specifically bats, which are allegedly consumed by humans. As a result, some individuals make the misguided decision to slaughter bats, mistakenly believing it helps curb the spread of the disease.

While the pandemic response has primarily focused on limiting the human outbreak, there are also significant concerns about the indiscriminate spraying of disinfectants to combat the virus. This raises the possibility that decomposition can be hindered or that more resistant bacteria and viruses may emerge.

While it is not wrong to prioritize human needs, humans are not the only ones affected by the pandemic. In fact, humans have always been responsible for a wide range of issues, particularly those that impact animals. For example, orangutans (and other wild animals) are driven out of their forest homes and forced into captivity because of human activities. These orangutans are often kept in cages for years.

Since the pandemic began, orangutans seem to have been overlooked. Given that 97% of their DNA is similar to that of humans, they are just as vulnerable to COVID-19, especially since this virus affects all living beings.

The conversion of forests for agricultural and urban purposes causes the displacement of orangutans from their natural habitats, leading to their domestication. As a result, they can no longer fulfill their vital role as caretakers of the forest, helping to maintain its health. This is the driving force behind the Borneo Orangutan Survival Foundation's (BOSF) rehabilitation efforts: to return orangutans, who have been uprooted from their natural environment, back to the forest, where they can once again fulfill their God-given duties.

So, what does this have to do with the COVID-19 pandemic? The Borneo Orangutan Survival Foundation (BOSF) currently cares for more than 425 orangutans across two rehabilitation centers. Since the virus entered Indonesia and began infecting people, BOSF has closed its doors to visitors and halted staff exchange programs. All procedures have been tightened.

Why? Because we are uncertain how fatal this virus could be to orangutans. Given their genetic similarity to humans, they are likely just as susceptible to COVID-19. Therefore, BOSF is not taking any chances. We have no choice but to prevent the virus from entering our premises. This is our top priority. As the saying goes, "Prevention is better than cure."

This situation is especially challenging, with the pandemic, the onset of an economic recession, and the rising costs of essential goods. Yet, the rehabilitation centers continue to house orangutans—state-owned wildlife that must be protected—whose health and welfare must be maintained despite dwindling funds and rising costs.

On the other hand, if the fortress that BOSF has built to prevent viruses from entering the rehabilitation centers collapses, the alarm bells will ring, and the warning lights will turn on. All orangutans and staff will have to undergo testing and monitoring. Costs will skyrocket, and the potential loss of animals will increase.

This reminds me of the story of the apostle Peter, who wanted to flee from Rome during the time when Emperor Nero was massacring Christians. On the way, Peter met Jesus, and He asked, "*Quo vadis, Domine?* Where are you going?"

If orangutans asked us the same question from their cages, "*Quo vadis?*"—meaning "Where are you going?"— "Will you leave us?" Our answer at BOSF is clear: We will keep fighting for orangutans and will not abandon them.

What about you, my friends? What's your answer?

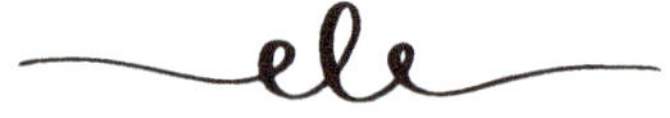

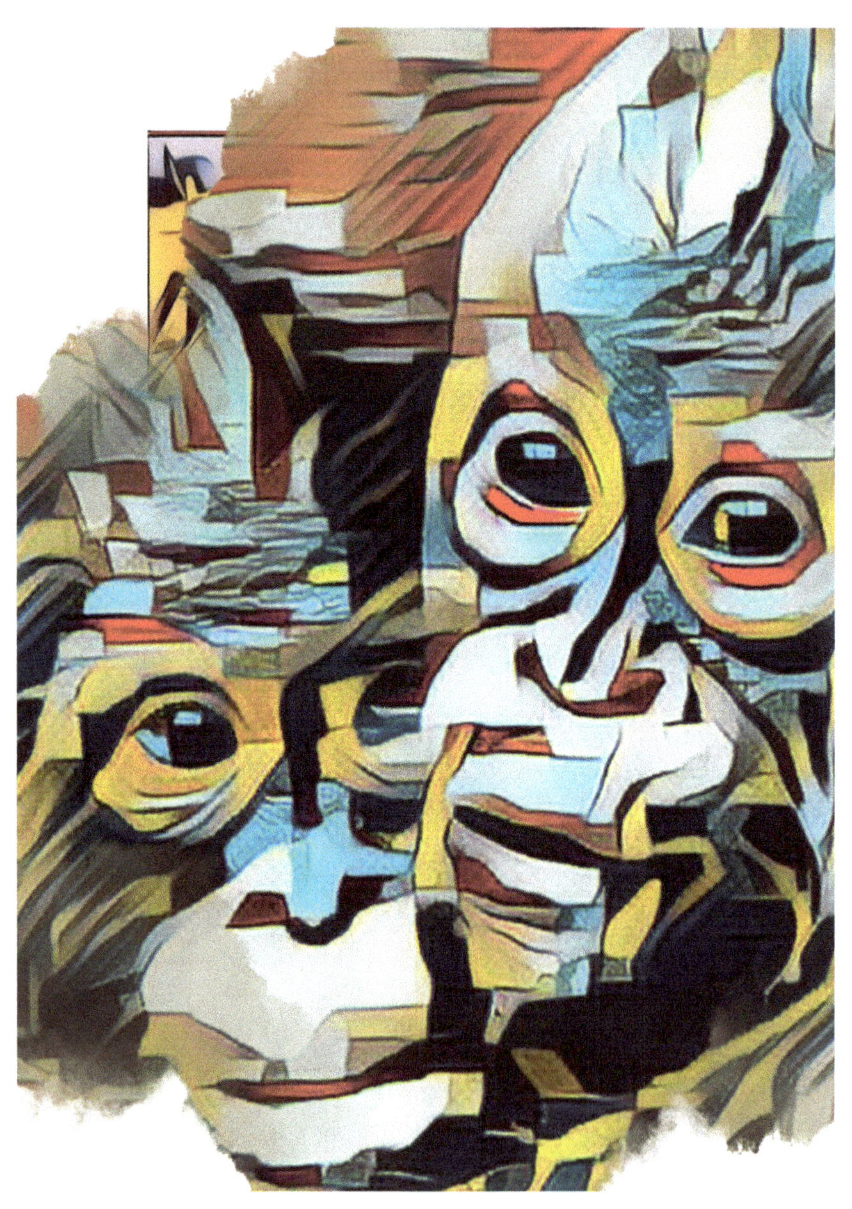

"Shouldn't orangutan conservation

happen in the forest?"

Chapter 29

Sit and Listen

Some time ago, a friend visited and said to me, "You should get involved in orangutan conservation, my friend." At that moment, I wondered, "Why would humans even want to care for orangutans?" Then he added, "Go and observe them. But don't look into the eyes of a baby orangutan, or you might fall in love."

Driven by my initial doubts and skepticism, I decided to take on his challenge.

When I first visited a rehabilitation center that cared for hundreds of large orangutans in enclosures, I was amazed. One word came to my mind to express my admiration: "*Wow!*" It was remarkable that they could care for so many orangutans, with the number housed at the center surpassing that of any zoo in the world. Yet, questions arose in my mind: "Is this the best way to save orangutans? Why are so many orangutans in cages, and full-grown at that? What is wrong with this situation? Didn't God create them to live in the forest? Shouldn't orangutan conservation happen in the forest?"

Then, I fell in love with orangutans for the first time when I looked into the eyes of a baby orangutan. Its gaze was so serene. Its body was so small, resembling that of a newborn human baby—frail and helpless, as if pleading for help, yet still hopeful. However, when my gaze shifted to the hundreds of adult orangutans trapped in cages, I couldn't help but wonder: What if I were in their position?

While it's true that the eyes of a baby orangutan can make us fall in love, what keeps us truly devoted—and motivates us to work and fight for them—is the look in the eyes of adult orangutans who have spent years in captivity. Eyes that seem to have lost their soul, yet tug at our heartstrings and inspire us to help restore life to them. This gaze has captivated me and kept me dedicated to this cause despite facing significant challenges. So, while falling in love is common, what's truly extraordinary is staying in love because it requires immense effort and commitment.

When baby orangutans are separated from their mothers' embrace, they are often kept by humans who mistakenly believe that keeping them as pets is a good idea. Driven by various motives, but under the guise of love, these individuals believe this is the right way to help orangutans. As a result, these babies become trapped in the "false love" of humans.

Do you realize that these babies would not be in the arms of their human caretakers if their mothers had not been killed? Orangutan mothers never abandon their young; they will fight with all their might and even risk their lives to protect them. Such is the bond that humans thoughtlessly break.

So, can love truly be built at the expense of another? People often struggle to distinguish between genuine love and the ego-driven desire to possess or even dominate, even though they frequently claim, "To love doesn't mean possessing."

When we at orangutan conservation rescue and educate these baby orangutans on how to live in nature—the life that God intended for them—hope for their return to the forest, their true home, begins to take shape. Their enthusiasm for learning to be wild fuels our passion for teaching them. As the Latin proverb states, "Non scholae, sed vitae discimus," meaning, "We learn not for school, but for life." Indeed, these orangutans learn so they can live in nature.

However, reality often falls short of this hope. Many rescued orangutans cannot return to their home in the forest because there are no forests for them to return to. After graduating from Forest School, they must return to sitting idly in enclosures. Their great energy and wild instincts—essential for survival in the wild—are once again confined to cages due to the lack of forests to release them into.

Imagine spending ten years working to rehabilitate hundreds of orangutans, only to have to shatter their hopes of returning home. Don't you think this job doesn't tear at our consciences and wound our hearts? Is this really the goal of rehabilitation? Why does this have to happen?

Amidst this, the Scriptures describe three important values of reference: faith, hope, and love. It is hope that ignites the spirit—the belief that, one day, they will return home. This reminds me of what Aristotle once said: "Hope is the dream of a waking man."

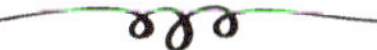

While contemplating the empty gaze of adult orangutans who had lost hope, I sat in the corner near a row of orangutan enclosures, silently trying to hear their whispers. I tried to listen to the wind, which seemed to carry their grievances: "Sit and listen; don't rush into action. It's better to simply sit, observe, and try to understand what they think and feel, and try to recognize the needs of the orangutans."

As I sat in silence, listening to the stillness, I was reminded of prayer—a dialogue with God that begins with listening to His voice. Because this was not the time to act based on our knowledge alone, assuming we knew best what the orangutans needed. Instead, it was a time to empathize and truly understand what the orangutans felt. This would strengthen our determination to persevere despite imperfect circumstances.

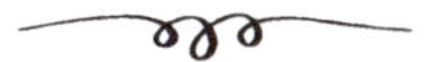

Before taking action to help orangutans, let us first listen to what they have to say and translate their hopes into real-world actions. This is possible if we are willing to sit, remain silent, and truly listen to them. Life is full of surprises. Do your part to the best of your ability, and then leave the rest to God, the owner of Life. As Martin Luther King Jr. said, "We must accept finite disappointment, but never lose infinite hope."

My father once said, "When you stop worrying about all the things you can't control, you will have enough time to change what you can control. Let today's troubles be enough for today." So, my friends, let us begin together with what we can do; we will break through the obstacles in our way and rekindle our enthusiasm. Isn't it true that, "No matter how many mistakes you make or how slow your progress, you are still way ahead of everyone who isn't trying?"

Let God open our hearts and minds and guide our actions. God clearly created orangutans to live in the forest, not in cages. If you still believe that orangutans are safer in cages, with all the reasons you claim as your love for them, perhaps you should consider changing their name—from "orangutan," meaning "forest people," to "cage people."

Enjoy the reflection!

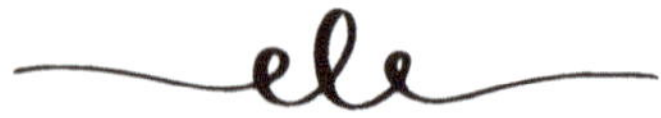

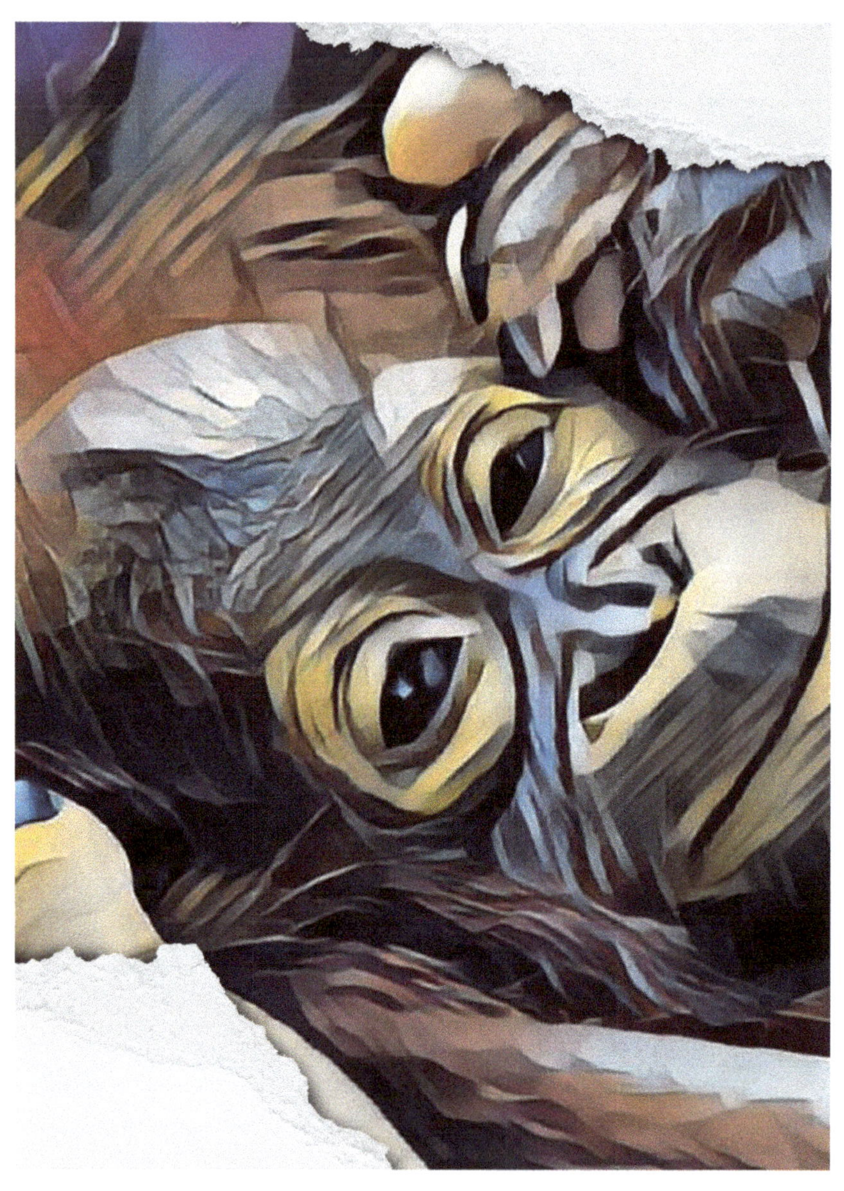

"Do we need orangutans,
or do orangutans need us?"

Chapter 30

Do We Need Orangutans?

"You're going to such great lengths just for orangutans," my children often comment, because they're familiar with my habit of wearing orangutan-themed attire. Almost every time I leave the house, I wear something promoting orangutan conservation, such as t-shirts, backpacks, hats, even suitcases with orangutan stickers attached—on top of our work uniform, which already displays the BOSF (Borneo Orangutan Survival Foundation) logo and a close-up image of an orangutan's face.

I do this as a reminder, a form of publicity, and part of an ongoing campaign (including BOSF's participation in various activities) to raise awareness about the importance of orangutans. My hope is that some people will notice, ask questions, and perhaps be inspired to own orangutan-themed items. So, in my opinion, "going to such great lengths for orangutans" (or as they say in Indonesian, '*sampai segitunya sama orangutan*') is not an exaggeration. If we don't take part in raising this nation's awareness of orangutans, then who will?

"When we organize an orangutan recognition day, known as 'Orangutan Day,' many people—not just my children—remark, "Why would you do that?" or "To *that* extent?!" or even, "Gosh, you've gone too far." Regardless of whether it evokes like or dislike, is considered exaggerated or overrated, or is subject to any other criticism, to me and my peers who remain dedicated to the conservation of orangutans and their habitats, having a day to commemorate orangutans is still important.

This is especially true since Orangutan Day was established out of concern for the chaotic state of orangutan conservation, caused by habitat fragmentation and land conversion, and further exacerbated by poaching (illegal hunting), which threatens and takes the lives of these endangered great apes, which play a crucial role in Indonesia's forests, particularly in Kalimantan (Indonesian Borneo) and Sumatra.

Orangutan Day is not about romanticizing the cuteness of baby orangutans. The fundamental question we ask each time we commemorate Orangutan Day is this: "Do we need orangutans, or do orangutans need us?"

This question is not just an empty slogan chanted on a podium or splashed across a banner. Rather, it is a topic for reflection—one that prompts us to analyze the current issues, determine the steps to take, and decide on the actions to pursue. Time is not on our side; we are already far behind. Whether we like it or not, we must try to catch up and rectify the damage that has been done to this planet, for the betterment of all its inhabitants. Remember, God did not just create humans on this earth; orangutans are also His creations.

On the other hand, Orangutan Day—no matter how big, grand, or festive—will have no meaning unless it is followed by real actions to save the orangutans. Let's consider this question: "Do we rescue orangutans to keep humans safe, or because they need help?"

Let's examine a few points that address the concerns above. In the forest, orangutans serve as an umbrella species. By protecting orangutans in their natural habitat, many other species will also be preserved and sheltered.

As frugivores (fruit-eating animals), orangutans can travel up to 100 hectares during the day to forage for fruits, and dispersing (and sowing) the seeds of the fruits they eat on the forest floor. At night, orangutans build nests to sleep in—an activity that is a unique phenomenon and an integral part of the natural laws of the universe. Orangutans construct their nests by parting the tree canopy and bending branches and twigs. This creates gaps between the leaves, allowing sunlight to stream through and reach the forest floor.

What are the benefits? The seeds of the fruits consumed by orangutans are scattered across the ground. With God's involvement, they sprout and grow into new trees. This process leads to efficient wood regeneration and maximizes the forest's role as a provider of environmental services.

The forest yields clean water, oxygen, timber, and non-timber forest products—all of which are beneficial to us humans.

If forests fail to thrive, sooner or later, we will lose the source of the oxygen we need to breathe. This highlights the importance of orangutans' role as gardeners of the forest, as expert planters in nature.

The next question to consider is: Would the extinction of orangutans be a problem for us? If the planet no longer had any orangutans, the balance of the ecosystem would be disrupted. The extinction of the orangutan is analogous to removing a single bolt from an airplane engine. The airplane can still fly, albeit in an imperfect condition. If we were informed about the absence of that one small bolt, would we still have the courage to board the plane? I'm sure no one would dare fly on it!

Orangutans are currently facing numerous threats. Poaching and habitat loss, as more of their forest homes are occupied and converted for human needs, have made their lives increasingly dire. It is our collective challenge and responsibility to ensure they continue living in the forests. For the future of our species and the preservation of our planet, we must not pass on orangutans merely in the form of legends and pictures to our future children and grandchildren.

We need orangutans as God originally placed them in their natural habitat, long before we existed. Will we deny what God has provided for our benefit on this earth?

Do not ask the swaying grass; ask within your hearts and minds.

Protecting orangutans in the forest is not for us to merely reflect on. So let's take action!

A version of this essay was published in thejakartapost.com on August 19, 2021 with the title "Do orangutans need humans, or vice versa?

Click to read: https://www.thejakartapost.com/academia/2021/08/18/do-orangutans-need-humans-or-vice-versa.html.

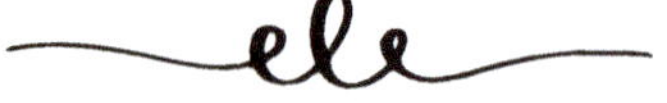

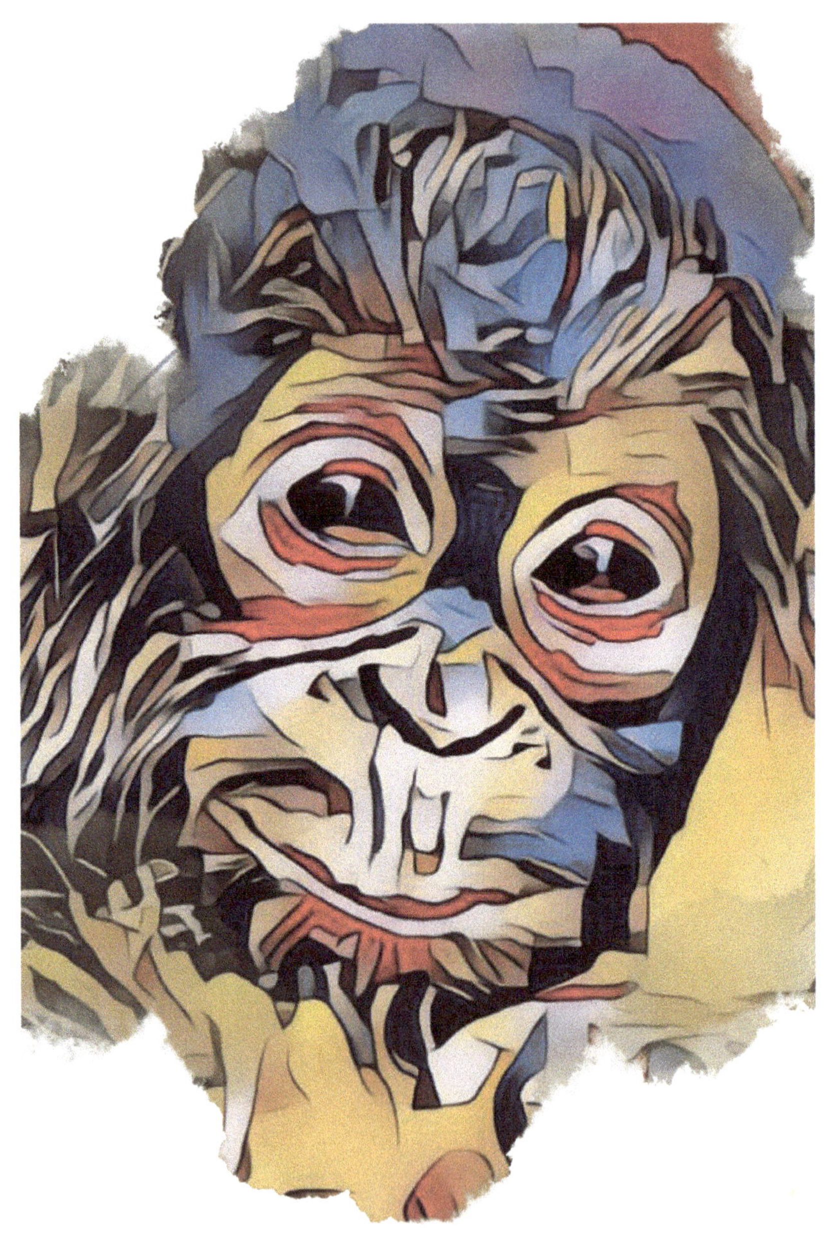

"He has appointed humankind
as His representatives on Earth,
to honor, protect, and care for His creation
—not to exploit, be cruel,
abuse, damage,
or, worse, destroy what He has created!"

Chapter 31

Let Us Reflect

When we discuss animal species, whether we realize it or not, we are often reminded of the creation of the earth and the sky as described in the Holy Book. This Sacred Text recounts how God first prepared the basic necessities for the survival of animals before creating them.

When we examine the evidence of creation around us, we discover how perfectly interconnected life is on Earth. We come to realize that God intentionally appointed and placed wildlife (such as orangutans and tigers) in forested areas for a specific purpose and that a symbiotic relationship exists between the animals and their environments, benefiting the entire planet—including humankind. In this context, orangutans, acting as stewards of the forest that is essential to life, play an integral role in maintaining a healthy ecosystem. They serve as guardians and caretakers of the areas they inhabit.

Let us take a look at how this symbiotic relationship works with orangutans. As an umbrella species, orangutans are not only beneficial to their ecosystem; they are, in fact, crucial to habitat conservation. They consume various types of fruit, disperse the seeds, and defecate on the ground. While traversing the forest, they open tree canopies, allowing sunlight to reach the forest floor, which helps germinate seeds into new plants. As these plants mature into a high-quality forest (a forest that is healthy, biodiverse, functionally intact, and capable of providing ecosystem services), the area will absorb carbon dioxide and provide the world with abundant oxygen, clean water, timber products, and non-timber forest products (such as those used in medicines). All of this is essential and used by all of us.

All wildlife in the forest has a role and is tasked with a duty from God, the Creator, to support all of His creation. They do not exist without meaning or significance. Yet, it is not uncommon to witness our kind (humans) arrogantly beat their chests and declare, "We homo sapiens are the only perfect creatures in God's creation, who have proven our merit as the most helpful to nature and its inhabitants." As a result, we believe humans are superior to other species. Is this the truth? In my opinion, it is time we re-examine this way of thinking.

Do we understand that God created the Earth and all its contents not by chance? I still remember when, one day in Sunday school, we were told that God created and placed humankind precisely on the very last day—even after He had created all the other creatures. Have we ever asked, "Why?" Have we ever thought about it, even once?

If only we were willing to temper our egos, we would understand that He is the sole holder and owner of the best plan for all humankind. He is the Creator of the heavens and the earth, the soil, water, and air, as well as various animals (including orangutans) and other creatures, all of which play a role in the well-being of human life from one generation to the next.

By being the last created, humans are, in fact, the weakest of all of God's creatures. Unfortunately, our inflated ego has become like dust on a mirror, clouding our hearts and consciences, causing us to fixate on the belief that all of His creation is under the control and command of humankind. This is deeply troubling.

If only we were willing to reflect on ourselves and understand the significance of why God created mankind in His image and likeness, we would realize that this was His intention—because He appointed humankind as His representatives on Earth, with the duty to respect, protect, and care for His creation—not to exploit, be cruel, abuse, damage, or, worse, destroy what He has created!

Isn't mistreating what He has bestowed upon us the same as mistreating ourselves? Isn't destroying His creation equivalent to ruining our relationship with the Supreme Owner? Remember that God is the Creator and absolute Owner of all things. So, before it's too late, let us come together and improve ourselves.

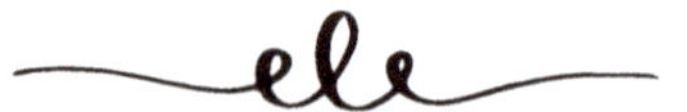

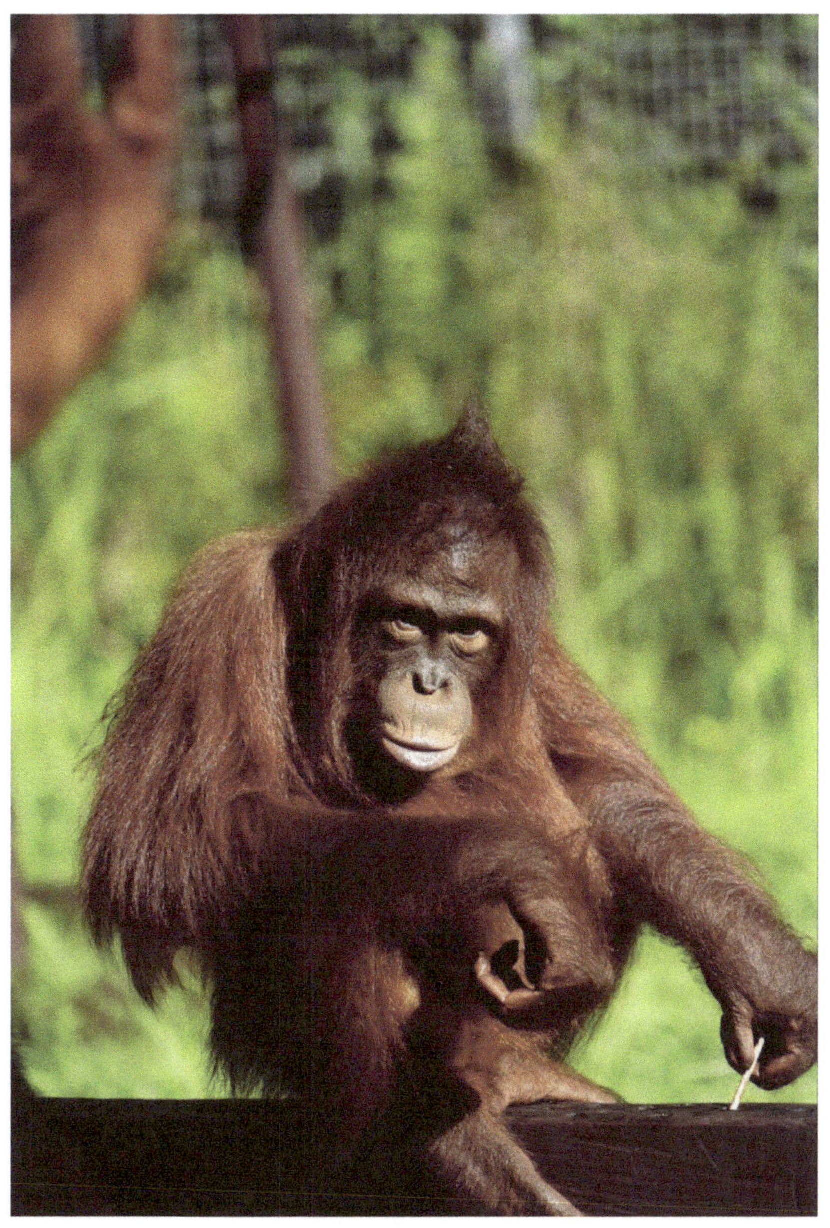

About the Author

Jamartin Sihite

is a long-time conservation activist with extensive experience and accomplishments in wildlife and habitat preservation in Indonesia, particularly in the conservation of Indonesia's endangered species: Komodo dragon (*Varanus komodoensis)* and Bornean orangutan (*Pongo pygmaeus).*

He was a lecturer at Trisakti University in Indonesia from 1992 to 2009. He was awarded a Master's and Doctorate degree in Environmental Sciences in 1993 and 2004, respectively. He later left academia to focus on conserving Indonesia's endangered species.

He held key positions in Putri Naga Komodo, the Orangutan Conservation Services Program (OCSP)—a project funded by USAID, and PT. Restorasi Habitat Orangutan Indonesia (RHOI).

In 2012, Jamartin assumed the role of CEO of the Borneo Orangutan Survival Foundation (BOSF). He has been the Chairman of the BOS Foundation since 2015.

Jamartin has received several awards for his contributions to orangutan conservation: the GRASP - Ian Redmond Conservation Award in 2015 for his work in orangutan reintroduction to their natural habitat, the McKenna-Travers Award for Compassionate Conservation in 2019 for his efforts in protecting Bornean orangutans and their habitat, and the Pongo Environmental Award in 2020 for his decades-long commitment of conserving orangutans and his role in ensuring the long-term survival of orangutans in Kalimantan.

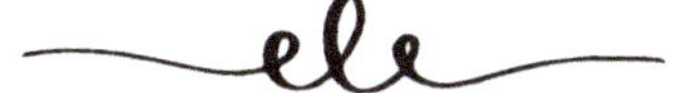

"Jamartin Sihite's personal experiences and imagined conversations with orangutans invite us all to reflect on our own values and actions. His short chapters should inspire everyone to contribute to safeguarding the survival of these great apes in their natural habitat and, thus, their unique ecosystem as well."

Prof. Dr. Carel van Schaik, Emeritus & Dr. Maria van Noordwijk
Department of Evolutionary Anthropology, Universität Zürich

"I thoroughly enjoyed this book. It was enlightening to get to know the real-life orangutan residents and understand the author's conservation philosophies. The writing was accessible and heartfelt, making it a rare and engaging read about orangutans conservation."

Helen Sullivan
Columnist and world news reporter @Guardian, also in @newyorker & @lrb

"The author has shared knowledge and stories of the conservation journey at Borneo Orangutan Survival Foundation (BOSF) in a way that is easily accessible to a wide audience. I hope more conservation experts can write in such a simple and engaging style, making their work comprehensible to the broader public, especially in Indonesia. This way, more people can become aware of and care for orangutans."

Prof. Jatna Supriatna, M.Sc., Ph.D
Professor of Conservation Biology, University of Indonesia.

"Jamartin Sihite's powerful storytelling doesn't just inform, it transforms. Silent Voices from the Jungle will spark a fire in your heart to take action, giving you a firsthand look at the impact of human actions on these gentle creatures and the delicate ecosystems they call home. By the time you finish, you'll feel an irresistible drive to walk the "silent path" alongside the author, carrying his mission forward."

Sharon Lynne
TV Director, Australia.

Contact & Book Order

Borneo Orangutan Survival Foundation (BOSF)
+62 811-9512-281
merchandise@orangutan.or.id
www.orangutan.or.id

  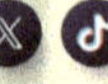  BOS Foundation

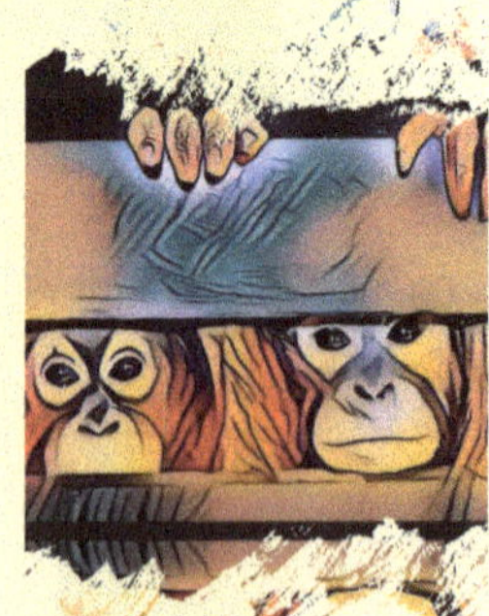